# Pearson
# Revise

T0351914

## Pearson Edexcel GCSE (9–1)
## Computer Science
## Revision Workbook

Series Consultant: Harry Smith

Authors: Cynthia Selby and Ann Weidmann

---

## Also available to support your revision:

Revise GCSE Study Skills Guide          9781292318875

The **Revise GCSE Study Skills Guide** is full of tried-and-trusted hints and tips for how to learn more effectively. It gives you techniques to help you achieve your best – throughout your GCSE studies and beyond!

Revise GCSE Revision Planner          9781292318868

The **Revise GCSE Revision Planner** helps you to plan and organise your time, step-by-step, throughout your GCSE revision. Use this book and wall chart to mastermind your revision.

---

**For the full range of Pearson revision titles across KS2, 11+, KS3, GCSE, Functional Skills, AS/A Level and BTEC visit:**

www.pearsonschools.co.uk/revise

Target grade **4-6**

### Question difficulty

Look at the Target grade range icon next to each exam-style question. It tells you how difficult the question is.

Published by Pearson Education Limited, 80 Strand, London, WC2R 0RL

www.pearsonschoolsandfecolleges.co.uk

Copies of official specifications for all Pearson qualifications may be found on the website: qualifications.pearson.com

Text and illustrations © Pearson Education Ltd 2021
Typeset and illustrated by Florence Production Ltd, UK
Produced by Florence Production Ltd, UK
Cover illustration by Pearson Education Ltd

The rights of Cynthia Selby and Ann Weidmann to be identified as authors of this work have been asserted
by them in accordance with the Copyright, Designs and Patents Act 1988.

Content written by David Waller is included.

First published 2021

24
14

**British Library Cataloguing in Publication Data**
A catalogue record for this book is available from the British Library

ISBN 9781292360058

Printed and bound in Great Britain by Bell and Bain Ltd, Glasgow

**Picture credits**
The publisher would like to thank the following for their kind permission to reproduce their photographs:

**Shutterstock**: Iakov Kalinin/Shutterstock 29

**Notes from the publisher**
1.  While the publishers have made every attempt to ensure that advice on the qualification and its assessment is accurate, the official
    specification and associated assessment guidance materials are the only authoritative source of information and should always be
    referred to for definitive guidance.

    Pearson examiners have not contributed to any sections in this resource relevant to examination papers for which they have responsibility.

2.  Pearson has robust editorial processes, including answer and fact checks, to ensure the accuracy of the content in this publication, and
    every effort is made to ensure this publication is free of errors. We are, however, only human, and occasionally errors do occur. Pearson
    is not liable for any misunderstandings that arise as a result of errors in this publication, but it is our priority to ensure that the content is
    accurate. If you spot an error, please do contact us at resourcescorrections@pearson.com so we can make sure it is corrected.

# Contents

- - - - - - - - - - -

Pearson Edexcel publishes Sample Assessment Material and the Specification on its website. This is the official content and this book should be used in conjunction with it. The questions have been written to help you practise every topic in the book. Remember: the real exam questions may not look like this.

# Using this book

## Code files

 You will see this icon next to some Topic 6 questions. It indicates that a question requires you to edit a Python code file. Python code model answers are provided for most Topic 6 questions.

These files can be found at **www.pearsonschools.co.uk/RevCS2021RW**, along with all code files mentioned in Timed test 2.

## Materials in the exam

In the Paper 1 exam there are no additional materials that you will need.

In the Paper 2 exam you will have:

- a computer workstation with appropriate programming language code editing software and tools, including an IDE that you are familiar with and that shows line numbers
- a 'STUDENT CODING' folder containing code and provided data files
- printed and electronic copies of the Programming Language Subset (PLS) document.

In revising Topic 6, you should set up the same environment. This will give you the best practice for the actual Paper 2 exam.

Remember, you do not have to learn all of the Python statements off by heart. You can look them up in the PLS, so do practise using it. You can find the PLS at **www.pearsonschools.co.uk/ RevCS2021RW**.

## Marking your work

Most answers can be found in the back of the book. Some questions in Topic 6 and Timed test 2 ask you to edit code files from the website as you would in the exam. The answers to these questions are alongside the question files on the Pearson website (see **Code files** note above).

Questions that require longer answers with more marks often have 'indicative' content in bullets in the answers, but you should also check the levels-based mark scheme (LBMS) at **www.pearsonschools.co.uk/RevCS2021RW** because there are multiple valid approaches you can take when answering them. You could answer the question very well using only a few items from the indicative content. An LBMS describes three levels of response. Each level is associated with a band of one or more marks.

- Paper 1 has one 6-mark 'essay' question which has an LBMS.
- In Paper 2 you will receive a mark for each accurate piece of code in your response (points-based) and a mark for the overall quality of your entire response (levels-based).

Each LBMS focuses on a different aspect of a candidate's response – solution design, good programming practices and functionality – all of which you should be doing when programming. A maximum of three marks can be awarded for each.

In Paper 2, one way to ensure you always gain marks using these LBMSs is to consider the design of your code and choice of programming statements. Use best programming practices with identifier names and readability techniques, and always make sure your program translates, even if it does not function perfectly.

# Decomposition and abstraction

**Target grade 1-3**

**1** A programmer is developing a game of noughts and crosses. The computer will play against the user. The programmer knows the game can be decomposed into many parts. One part is needed to display the board.

Name **three** other parts of the decomposed solution. **(3 marks)**

1 ....................................................................................................................

....................................................................................................................

2 ....................................................................................................................

....................................................................................................................

3 ....................................................................................................................

....................................................................................................................

**Target grade 1-3**

**2** A programmer is developing a server application that keeps track of books in a library.

Complete the table by inserting a tick to indicate if the item in the left-most column must be considered or if it can be abstracted away during the development of the application. **(5 marks)**

> In this question, you must consider how important each item in the left-most column is for identifying books in a library. If you, as a person, would need that information to find a book or set of books, then the application will need that same information.

| Item | Must be kept | Can be abstracted away |
|------|--------------|------------------------|
| The colour of the cover | | |
| The International Standard Book Number (ISBN) | | |
| The shelf location | | |
| The subject area | | |
| The type of cover (hardback or paperback) | | |

# Using subprograms

**Target grade 1-3**

**1** Define the term 'subprogram'. **(1 mark)**

......................................................................................................................................

......................................................................................................................................

**Target grade 7-9**

**2** Subprograms are both decompositions and abstractions.
Discuss the characteristics of subprograms that make them both
a decomposition and an abstraction. **(6 marks)**

> In this question, you need to recall what decomposition and abstraction
> are. Make some notes in the margins or on scrap paper. Next, recall
> the characteristics of subprograms. Identify the relationship between
> abstraction and subprograms and the relationship between decomposition
> and subprograms.

......................................................................................................................................

......................................................................................................................................

......................................................................................................................................

......................................................................................................................................

......................................................................................................................................

......................................................................................................................................

......................................................................................................................................

......................................................................................................................................

......................................................................................................................................

......................................................................................................................................

......................................................................................................................................

......................................................................................................................................

......................................................................................................................................

......................................................................................................................................

# Algorithms: flowcharts

**Target grade 1-3**

1  There are two items that every complete flowchart should have. Draw and label the two items.

**(2 marks)**

**Target grade 4-6**

2  Describe the purpose of this symbol:

**(2 marks)**

.......................................................................................................

.......................................................................................................

.......................................................................................................

**Target grade 1-3**

3  Draw a flowchart to initialise variable(s), accept a number from the user, double it and display it back to the user.

**(2 marks)**

> This question sets out the order for the algorithm solution. Be sure to follow it and use the correct symbols for each step.

# Algorithms: selection

1  Identify the number of outputs required by a selection symbol in a flowchart.   **(1 mark)**

☐ **A** Exactly one

☐ **B** Exactly two

☐ **C** One or more

☐ **D** Two or more

2  Here is a flowchart for an algorithm that displays an output, based on a letter typed in by the user. The user input must be a capital letter.

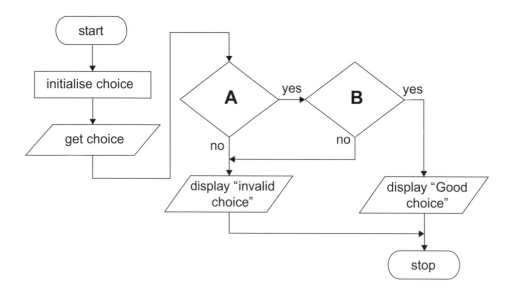

Give the statements that should replace A and B to make the algorithm function correctly.   **(4 marks)**

In this question, focus on what you know about the selection symbol and how its contents should be constructed. Do a double check to make sure that it functions correctly with the statements you are providing.

A ..........................................................................................................................

..........................................................................................................................

B ..........................................................................................................................

..........................................................................................................................

# Algorithms: repetition

1   Here is a flowchart for an algorithm.         **(2 marks)**

```
                    ┌─────────┐
                    │  start  │
                    └─────────┘
                         │
              ┌──────────────────────┐              ┌──────────────┐
              │ initialise numItems,  │──────┐       │     get      │
              │ itemPrice, totalPrice │      │       │   numItems    │
              └──────────────────────┘      │       └──────────────┘
                         │                   │              │
                    ╱ is ╲                   │         ╱   is    ╲
          yes      ╱ totalPrice ╲    no       └──── yes ╱ numItems  ╲
         ┌────────╱  >= 100?    ╲──┐          ┌──────╱   == 0?     ╲
         │        ╲            ╱   │          │      ╲            ╱
         │         ╲          ╱    │          │       ╲   │ no  ╱
         │                         │          │      ┌──────────────┐
   ┌──────────────────────┐        │          │      │     get      │
   │ totalPrice = totalPrice │      │          │      │   itemPrice   │
   │ (totalPrice / 100 * 10) │      │          │      └──────────────┘
   └──────────────────────┘        │          │              │
         │                         │          │   ┌──────────────────────┐
   ┌──────────────────────┐        │          │   │ totalPrice = totalPrice + │
   │  display "Please      │        │          │   │      itemPrice         │
   │  pay:" + totalPrice   │        │          │   └──────────────────────┘
   └──────────────────────┘        │          │              │
         │                         │          │   ┌──────────────────────┐
    ┌─────────┐                    │          └───│  decrement numItems   │
    │  stop   │                    │              └──────────────────────┘
    └─────────┘
```

> The word 'decrement' is used in this flowchart. It means to subtract one.

**Target grade 7-9**

  (a)   Describe the function of this algorithm.        **(2 marks)**

.............................................................................................................

.............................................................................................................

.............................................................................................................

.............................................................................................................

**Target grade 4-6**

  (b)   Examine the selection symbols carefully.
        Give the contents of the selection symbol that works as a repetition.      **(1 mark)**

> This question is asking you to remember that a backward arrow to the top of a selection symbol is a loop. Find that selection symbol and write its contents in the space provided.

.............................................................................................................

.............................................................................................................

# Algorithms: iteration

1  An algorithm is needed to process a two-dimensional data structure storing integer numbers. Here is the data structure holding the integer numbers.

```
numTable = [[10, 20, 30, 40, 50],
            [60, 70, 80, 90, 100],
            [110, 120, 130, 140, 150]]
```

The algorithm must meet these requirements:

- Add up the numbers in each row.
- Display the total for each row.
- Create a grand total by adding the totals from each row.
- Display the grand total for the whole data structure.

Output from the algorithm:

```
Row total: 150
Row total: 400
Row total: 650
Grand total: 1200
```

Draw a flowchart to show this algorithm.

**(7 marks)**

> The data structure in this question is two-dimensional. You will need one iteration loop to go down the row dimension. Then, inside the row loop, you will need another iteration loop to go across each column. This means you will need to nest one loop inside the other. You should have two selection symbols, both with backward arrows, to do the iterations.

# Variables and constants

**1** Program code makes use of variables and constants.

**Target grade 1-3**

(a) Define what is meant by a variable.  **(2 marks)**

.................................................................................................................................

.................................................................................................................................

.................................................................................................................................

**Target grade 4-6**

(b) Constants are written in all upper case and variables are written in camel case. Describe **one** other way that a constant differs from a variable.  **(2 marks)**

.................................................................................................................................

.................................................................................................................................

**Target grade 1-3**

(c) State **one** reason variables and constants should be given meaningful names.  **(1 mark)**

.................................................................................................................................

.................................................................................................................................

**Target grade 4-6**

(d) The algorithm shown below allows the user to type in guesses until the correct number is entered.  **(6 marks)**

```
1    mysteryNumber = 6
2    correct = False
3    while (correct == False):
4        guess = int (input ("Enter a guess: "))
5        if (guess == mysteryNumber):
6            correct = True
```

Complete the table to show the variables used and why they are used in the program.

> Read the algorithm carefully to identify the variables and to understand why they have been used. The first one has been done for you.

| Variable | Use within the program |
|----------|------------------------|
| mysteryNumber | This is used to hold the number which must be guessed. |
| | |
| | |
| | |

# Arrays

**Target grade 4-6**

**1** (a) Define the term 'array'. **(2 marks)**

.................................................................................................................................

.................................................................................................................................

.................................................................................................................................

(b) Jack has taken his temperature every day for a week and has stored the readings in an array named 'temp'.

The data for the week has already been entered and stored in 'temp'.

Here is the 'temp' data structure and its contents.

```
temp = [36.5, 36.8, 37.1, 36.7, 36.5, 37.2, 36.9]
```

**Target grade 1-3**

(i) State the index of the last item in temp. **(1 mark)**

.................................................................................................................................

**Target grade 4-6**

(ii) Give the value at temp[3]. **(1 mark)**

.................................................................................................................................

**Target grade 1-3**

(iii) Give the name for the programming construct needed to traverse every item in a data structure. **(1 mark)**

.................................................................................................................................

**Target grade 1-3**

**2** The figure shows a black and white bitmap image.

The image can be encoded using 0 to represent black pixels and 1 to represent white pixels.

Complete the matrix below to show how the pixel data could be stored in a two-dimensional array.

The first row has been done for you. **(3 marks)**

|   | 0 | 1 | 2 | 3 |
|---|---|---|---|---|
| **0** | 1 | 0 | 0 | 1 |
| **1** |   |   |   |   |
| **2** |   |   |   |   |
| **3** |   |   |   |   |

Notice in this grid that represents an array, the row and column indices have been shaded. This clearly indicates that they do not form part of the array and are not stored in memory. If you are asked to draw an array, remember, you must either leave the row and column indices off completely or make sure there is not a border around them.

# Records

**Target grade 4-6**

1  (a)  Both records and arrays are data structures.

State **one** similarity and **one** difference between arrays and records.    **(2 marks)**

Similarity  ................................................................................................................

................................................................................................................

Difference  ................................................................................................................

................................................................................................................

(b)  Reuben is opening a cattery to look after animals when their owners go on holiday.

He wants to store information about the cats in a suitable data structure. The data is shown in the table below.

| Name | Gender | Weight (kg) | Number of days | Special diet? |
|------|--------|-------------|----------------|---------------|
| Dottie | F | 3.2 | 6 | N |
| Jack | M | 4.2 | 7 | Y |
| Tom | M | 5.1 | 4 | N |

**Target grade 7-9**

(i)  Describe **one** reason records are a more suitable data structure for storing this data than arrays.    **(2 marks)**

> This question requires you to compare records and arrays in the context of this scenario. Be sure to include connecting words, such as 'on the other hand' or 'whereas', in your response and address both records and arrays.

................................................................................................................

................................................................................................................

................................................................................................................

................................................................................................................

**Target grade 1-3**

(ii)  State the reason why the column heading row in the table is coloured grey.    **(1 mark)**

................................................................................................................

................................................................................................................

................................................................................................................

................................................................................................................

# Arithmetic and relational operators

**1** Relational operators are used in algorithms and programs.

**Target grade 1-3**

(a) State the purpose of relational operators.     **(1 mark)**

........................................................................................................................

........................................................................................................................

........................................................................................................................

........................................................................................................................

**Target grade 4-6**

(b) Name a programming construct that uses a relational operator.     **(1 mark)**

........................................................................................................................

........................................................................................................................

........................................................................................................................

........................................................................................................................

**Target grade 4-6**

**2** Complete the table below by evaluating each of the statements listed and stating whether it is True or False.

The first one has been done for you.     **(4 marks)**

> You first need to work out the results of the calculations and then compare them using the operators.

| Statement | True/False |
|---|---|
| 14 // 3 < 4 | False |
| 2**3 >= 8 | |
| 12 + 6 / 2 == 15 | |
| 6 * (8 / 2) > (6 * 8) / 2 | |
| 23 % 6 != 5 | |

# Logical operators

1 Complete the table below to show the output of each algorithm.
The first solution has been completed for you.

(3 marks)

> Read and work through the algorithms carefully and write the expected outcome in the second column.

| Algorithm | Output |
| --- | --- |
| ```number = 3``` <br> ```if ((number > 0) and (number < 2)):``` <br> ```    print ("Within range")``` <br> ```else:``` <br> ```    print ("Out of range")``` | Out of range |
| ```number = 6``` <br> ```if ((not (number == 3)) or (number != 5)):``` <br> ```    print ("Number is acceptable")``` <br> ```else:``` <br> ```    print ("Number is not acceptable")``` | |
| ```colour = "red"``` <br> ```size = "m"``` <br> ```price = 25``` <br> ```if ((colour == "blue") or``` <br> ```        (colour == "red") and``` <br> ```        (size == "m")):``` <br> ```    print ("This would be OK")``` <br> ```else:``` <br> ```    print ("Not OK")``` | |
| ```number1 = 6``` <br> ```number2 = 9``` <br> ```if (((number1 <= 9) or (number2 >= 10)) and``` <br> ```        (not(number1 * number2 < 50)) and``` <br> ```        (number2 - number1 == 3)):``` <br> ```    print ("These numbers are OK")``` <br> ```else:``` <br> ```    print ("Not OK")``` | |

# Determining correct output

1  In this algorithm, names is an array of strings implemented as a list.

```
1    index = 1
2    unique = True
3    loginName = ""
4    names = ["aaa", "bbb", "ccc"]
5
6    firstName = input ("Please enter the first name. ")
7    familyName = input ("Please enter the family name. ")
8    strYear = input ("Please enter the intake year e.g. 2010. ")
9    tutorGroup = input ("Please enter the tutor group. ")
10
11   loginName = strYear[2] + strYear[3] + familyName + \
12               firstName[0] + tutorGroup
13
14   while ((unique == True) and (index < len (names))):
15       for check in range (len (names)):
16           if (names[check] == loginName):
17               unique = False
18           else:
19               index = index + 1
20
21   if (unique):
22       print (loginName + " is unique. ")
23   else:
24       print (loginName + " is already used. ")
```

**Target grade 4-6**

(a)  State the purpose of this algorithm.

(2 marks)

...........................................................................................................................

...........................................................................................................................

**Target grade 1-3**

(b)  State the inputs required by the algorithm.

(4 marks)

...........................................................................................................................

...........................................................................................................................

**Target grade 4-6**

(c)  An array named 'names' is used in the algorithm.
State the role of the variable named 'check'.

(1 mark)

...........................................................................................................................

...........................................................................................................................

**Target grade 4-6**

(d)  State the output for this input: Rosie Cooper in the intake year of 2018
and in the tutor group Blue. Assume her login name is unique.

(5 marks)

...........................................................................................................................

# Using trace tables

1  Here is an algorithm.

```
1   numList = [5, 9, 13, 2]
2   target = 13
3   found = False
4
5   for index in range (len (numList)):
6       if (target == numList[index]):
7           found = True
8
9   if (found):
10      print ("The item is in the list.")
11  else:
12      print ("The item is not in the list.")
```

> Before you start, read through the algorithm very carefully. Make sure that you understand the structure of the logic. It is OK if you do not know exactly what the code is supposed to do. The trace table will help with that.

Target grade 1-3

(a) Identify the data stucture used to store the number in the list.                    **(1 mark)**

.................................................................................................................................

Target grade 7-9

(b) Complete the trace table to show the execution of the algorithm.
    The target item is 13. You may not need to fill in all the rows in the table.        **(6 marks)**

> Remember, each row is a pass through the loop. When the loop terminates, you move to the next row.

| target | found | index | numList[index] | output |
|--------|-------|-------|----------------|--------|
|        |       |       |                |        |
|        |       |       |                |        |
|        |       |       |                |        |
|        |       |       |                |        |
|        |       |       |                |        |
|        |       |       |                |        |
|        |       |       |                |        |

**Had a go** ☐ **Nearly there** ☐ **Nailed it!** ☐

# Errors that can occur in programs

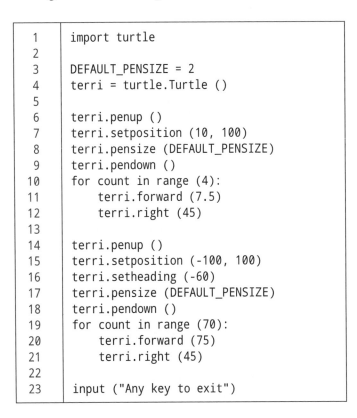

**Target grade 4-6**

**1** Here is a drawing of a turtle graphics image.
The algorithm has these requirements:

- Upper left corner of square is at (100, 100).
- Upper vertex of triangle is at (−100, 100).
- All sides are 75 units.
- The triangle's lines are twice as thick as the square's lines.
- No lines are overdrawn.

Here is the first attempt at an algorithm to produce this image.
The algorithm has five logic errors.

```
1    import turtle
2
3    DEFAULT_PENSIZE = 2
4    terri = turtle.Turtle ()
5
6    terri.penup ()
7    terri.setposition (10, 100)
8    terri.pensize (DEFAULT_PENSIZE)
9    terri.pendown ()
10   for count in range (4):
11       terri.forward (7.5)
12       terri.right (45)
13
14   terri.penup ()
15   terri.setposition (-100, 100)
16   terri.setheading (-60)
17   terri.pensize (DEFAULT_PENSIZE)
18   terri.pendown ()
19   for count in range (70):
20       terri.forward (75)
21       terri.right (45)
22
23   input ("Any key to exit")
```

> Read through the code carefully and execute it in your head. This will give you an idea of what it should do. For each line number given, identify what the algorithm should be doing at that point. From there you can construct a line of code.

Complete the table to provide corrections for the errors. **(5 marks)**

| Error line number | Correction |
|:---:|---|
| 7 | |
| 11 | |
| 12 | |
| 17 | |
| 19 | |

# Linear search

1   A linear search is one algorithm that can be used to locate a target in a data structure.

**Target grade 4-6**

(a)   Describe how a linear search algorithm works.     **(2 marks)**

..............................................................................................................................

..............................................................................................................................

..............................................................................................................................

..............................................................................................................................

**Target grade 4-6**

(b)   Define the term 'brute-force algorithm'.     **(1 mark)**

..............................................................................................................................

..............................................................................................................................

..............................................................................................................................

..............................................................................................................................

**Target grade 7-9**

(c)   Here is one algorithm for a linear search:

```
1   colours = ["red", "green", "blue", "yellow", "pink",
2               "orange"]
3   target = "black"
4   found = False
5   for item in colours:
6       if (item == target):
7           found = True
8
9   if (found):
10      print ("Found the colour")
11  else:
12      print ("Colour not found")
```

> When judging the suitability of an algorithm, look for the number of items that must be accessed, in this case the 'for…in' loop on line 5.

Explain **one** reason this linear search algorithm is not suitable for long lists.     **(2 marks)**

..............................................................................................................................

..............................................................................................................................

..............................................................................................................................

..............................................................................................................................

# Binary search

**Target grade 4-6**

**1** A binary search is described as a 'divide and conquer' algorithm.

Describe the features of a binary search algorithm that make it a 'divide and conquer' approach.

**(2 marks)**

.......................................................................................................................

.......................................................................................................................

.......................................................................................................................

.......................................................................................................................

**Target grade 1-3**

**2** Here is a list of colours.

| Red | Yellow | Green | Blue | Pink |
|-----|--------|-------|------|------|

A binary search is not a suitable algorithm for a very short list like this one.

State **one** other reason that a binary search is not a suitable algorithm for use on this list of data.

**(1 mark)**

.......................................................................................................................

**Target grade 7-9**

**3** A student makes the following list of his friends.

| Ahmad | Ava | Emma | Josiah | Mateo | Maya | Paru | Stephen | Zoey |
|-------|-----|------|--------|-------|------|------|---------|------|

Complete the table below to show the steps of a binary search to find the name 'Stephen'.

**(3 marks)**

> You should include the calculation to find the index of the median item and show the median item. Copy the new sublist into the first column for the next pass.

| Sublist | Median calculation | Median item |
|---------|--------------------|-------------|
| Ahmad Ava Emma Josiah Mateo Maya Paru Stephen Zoey | | |
| | | |
| | | |

# Bubble sort

**1** Here is a list of numbers that must be sorted.

Complete the table to show the passes of a bubble sort to sort the numbers into ascending order.     **(6 marks)**

| | 20 | 15 | 3 | 13 | 9 | 2 | 6 |
|---|---|---|---|---|---|---|---|
| **Pass 1** | | | | | | | |
| **Pass 2** | | | | | | | |
| **Pass 3** | | | | | | | |
| **Pass 4** | | | | | | | |
| **Pass 5** | | | | | | | |
| **Pass 6** | | | | | | | |

> In the exam, you can use the margins for rough work, so you may make each pass and double check it before writing it into the table. Remember to write clearly and only put one response into each cell of the table.

**2** Here is a list of numbers that must be sorted.

| −12 | 0 | −2 | 4 | 7 | 5 | 9 |
|---|---|---|---|---|---|---|

State the number of swaps required to completely sort the list in ascending order.     **(1 mark)**

..................................................................................................................................

**3** Here is a list of names.

| Lola | Inez | Gwynn | Fatima | Evelyn | Charlie | Ali |
|---|---|---|---|---|---|---|

State the number of passes to completely sort the list in descending order.     **(1 mark)**

> Normally, when you sort words you use alphabetical order. However, this question has stated that you are sorting in descending order, which is reverse alphabetical. Read the questions carefully, so you do not make a mistake.

..................................................................................................................................

# Merge sort

**Target grade 7-9**

**1** The merge sort algorithm divides up a list into smaller and smaller sections and then sorts them into order before putting them back together again.

Describe the advantage of using this technique.

**(2 marks)**

.................................................................................................................................

.................................................................................................................................

.................................................................................................................................

.................................................................................................................................

**Target grade 7-9**

**2** Use a merge sort to put the data shown below into ascending order.

Draw a diagram to show all the stages of the process.

**(6 marks)**

| 33 | 25 | 46 | 2 | 8 | 69 | 9 |
|----|----|----|---|---|----|---|

# Efficiency of algorithms

**Target grade 1-3**

1 Describe **one** reason a bubble sort is preferable to a merge sort for students to use in GCSE Computer Science classes. **(2 marks)**

> This question specifies the context of the classroom. Your response needs to include that context. The question is asking for a comparison response. Talk about both bubble and merge sort in the context of them being used by beginner programmers.

........................................................................................................................

........................................................................................................................

........................................................................................................................

........................................................................................................................

**Target grade 7-9**

2 (a) When searching a list of 100 items, the largest number of comparisons a linear search would have to make would be 100.

Complete the steps to show that the maximum possible number of comparisons made using a binary search of the same list would be 7.

Show your working. **(4 marks)**

........................................................................................................................

........................................................................................................................

........................................................................................................................

........................................................................................................................

........................................................................................................................

........................................................................................................................

**Target grade 4-6**

(b) A binary search is generally more efficient than a linear search. However, this is not always the case.

Describe **one** reason using a linear search may be quicker than using a binary search in some circumstances. **(2 marks)**

........................................................................................................................

........................................................................................................................

........................................................................................................................

........................................................................................................................

# Logical operators

**Target grade 4-6**

1   Truth tables are used to show how digital output relates to input.

Complete the truth table for the OR statement.                                                    **(3 marks)**

| Input | | Output |
|---|---|---|
| 0 | 0 | |
| | | |
| | | |
| | | |

**Target grade 4-6**

2   A conveyer belt in a factory can be turned on by either switch A or B.
To ensure the safety of the workers there is also an override switch that
must be in the off position before the belt will move.

(a)   Construct a logical statement to represent the logic of this behaviour,
using the symbols A, B and C.                                                                      **(2 marks)**

.......................................................................................................................

.......................................................................................................................

(b)   Complete the truth table for this statement where P represents the movement
of the belt.                                                                                                       **(4 marks)**

| A | B | C | P |
|---|---|---|---|
| | | | |
| | | | |
| | | | |
| | | | |
| | | | |
| | | | |
| | | | |
| | | | |

> Make sure when completing input values for truth tables that you get all
> unique combinations of the inputs. You could enter the digits in column A,
> B and C as if you were counting in binary from 000 to 111.

# Using binary

**Target grade 4-6**

**1** Explain **one** reason why all instructions and data used by a computer are represented in binary.

**(3 marks)**

..............................................................................................................................

..............................................................................................................................

..............................................................................................................................

..............................................................................................................................

..............................................................................................................................

..............................................................................................................................

**Target grade 4-6**

**2** Four binary digits are used to represent a colour in a graphics program.
Identify the number of different colours that can be represented.

**(1 mark)**

☐ **A** 4

☐ **B** 8

☐ **C** 16

☐ **D** 32

**Target grade 4-6**

**3** Three binary digits are used to represent a character.
Give the different combinations of digits that are possible.

**(3 marks)**

> You should write down all of the unique combinations where each digit can be either a 0 or a 1.

000, 001, ................................................................................................

..............................................................................................................................

**Target grade 1-3**

**4** The denary value of each binary digit is given by its place value. Complete the table below to show the denary value represented by each of the digits.

**(1 mark)**

> The denary value is given by the binary digit multiplied by its place value.

| 1 | 0 | 1 | 1 |
|---|---|---|---|
|   |   |   |   |

**Target grade 1-3**

**5** Describe a 'bit'.

**(2 marks)**

..............................................................................................................................

..............................................................................................................................

..............................................................................................................................

# Unsigned integers

Target grade 4-6

**1** Convert the denary number 199 into an 8-bit binary number.

(2 marks)

> Remember to compare the denary number with the binary place value and calculate the remainder.
>
> You can use spare paper for your working out.

.................................................................................................................

.................................................................................................................

.................................................................................................................

.................................................................................................................

Target grade 4-6

**2** Convert the 8-bit binary number 1001 0111 into a denary number.

(2 marks)

> Remember to multiply the binary digits by their place values. You could use a table to help you to do this.

.................................................................................................................

.................................................................................................................

.................................................................................................................

.................................................................................................................

Target grade 1-3

**3** Explain **one** reason why the denary number 256 cannot be represented in an 8-bit binary pattern.

(2 marks)

.................................................................................................................

.................................................................................................................

.................................................................................................................

.................................................................................................................

# Two's complement signed integers

**Target grade 4-6**

**1** Convert the denary number −54 to 8-bit binary two's complement representation. **(3 marks)**

> Be sure that your logic for the conversion steps is clear. Indicate which is a positive number, which is a negative number, the flipping stage and the adding stage.

.............................................................................................................................

.............................................................................................................................

.............................................................................................................................

.............................................................................................................................

**Target grade 7-9**

**2** A student was asked to convert the 8-bit binary number 0101 0111 to 8-bit binary two's complement representation. The student's answer was 1011 1001.

Explain whether the answer is correct or incorrect. **(3 marks)**

> This type of question requires you to make a choice and then provide a justification. State your choice clearly. Be sure to make two linked points in your justification.

.............................................................................................................................

.............................................................................................................................

.............................................................................................................................

.............................................................................................................................

.............................................................................................................................

**Target grade 4-6**

**3** Give the denary value of the 8-bit two's complement number 1110 1111. **(3 marks)**

.............................................................................................................................

.............................................................................................................................

.............................................................................................................................

.............................................................................................................................

.............................................................................................................................

# Binary addition

**Target grade 4-6**

1  Add the following 8-bit binary numbers.
   Give your answer in 8-bit binary form.                                    **(2 marks)**

| 0 | 1 | 0 | 1 | 0 | 1 | 1 | 1 |
| 0 | 1 | 0 | 1 | 1 | 1 | 1 | 1 |

_____

_____

**Target grade 7-9**

2  A student was asked to add the 8-bit binary numbers, 0101 0111 and 0100 1010.
   Their answer was 1011 0001. Was their answer correct or incorrect?         **(3 marks)**

> In this question you must make a choice. State whether the given answer is
> correct or not. Then, use your working to justify your choice.

.................................................................................................................

.................................................................................................................

.................................................................................................................

.................................................................................................................

3  Electrical circuits do not understand about signed numbers. They just add binary
   patterns.

**Target grade 4-6**

   (a)  Complete the table to add the binary patterns.                        **(2 marks)**

| O | O | O | 1 | 1 | 1 | O | O |
| 1 | 1 | 1 | O | O | 1 | O | O |
|   |   |   |   |   |   |   |   |

**Target grade 4-6**

   (b)  Assume the 8-bit binary pattern in the first row represents a signed integer.
        Give the denary value for the 8-bit binary pattern.                    **(1 mark)**

.................................................................................................................

**Target grade 4-6**

   (c)  Assume the 8-bit binary pattern in the second row represents a signed
        integer in two's complement format. Give the denary value for the 8-bit
        binary pattern.                                                        **(1 mark)**

.................................................................................................................

# Logical and arithmetic shifts

**Target grade 1-3**

1   Describe **one** difference between a logical and an arithmetic shift.    **(2 marks)**

......................................................................................................................

......................................................................................................................

......................................................................................................................

......................................................................................................................

**Target grade 1-3**

2   Here is a bit pattern 1110 1100. Complete the table to show the result of applying each type of shift to this bit pattern.    **(4 marks)**

| Shift | Result |
|---|---|
| Logical right shift of four places | |
| Logical left shift of two places | |
| Arithmetic right shift of three places | |
| Arithmetic left shift of one place | |

**Target grade 7-9**

3   (a)   Complete the following table to show the effect of performing a logical shift right of two places on the binary number 1010 1101. State the decimal equivalent of each of the binary numbers.    **(3 marks)**

> You must carry out the logical shift and also convert the numbers to decimal. This will help you to check that you have carried out the shift correctly.

| Binary number | 1010 1101 | Decimal equivalent | |
|---|---|---|---|
| Binary number after a two-place logical shift right | | Decimal equivalent | |

   (b)   Explain the results shown in the table.    **(2 marks)**

> You should state the divisor being used in a logical shift of two places and also state any difference between the actual result and what would be expected if that divisor were used on the decimal number.

......................................................................................................................

......................................................................................................................

......................................................................................................................

......................................................................................................................

# Overflow

**Target grade 1-3**

**1** Define the term 'overflow'.                                                                                    **(2 marks)**

......................................................................................................................................

......................................................................................................................................

......................................................................................................................................

......................................................................................................................................

......................................................................................................................................

**Target grade 1-3**

**2** State two consequences of an overflow error.                                                                   **(2 marks)**

......................................................................................................................................

......................................................................................................................................

......................................................................................................................................

**Target grade 1-3**

**3** Complete the table to show the result of adding the two 8-bit binary patterns.                                 **(3 marks)**

| 1 | O | 1 | O | 1 | O | 1 | O |
|---|---|---|---|---|---|---|---|
| 1 | O | 1 | O | 1 | O | 1 | O |
|   |   |   |   |   |   |   |   |

**Target grade 4-6**

**4** Give the result of adding the 8-bit binary patterns 0110 1100 and 1100 0101.                                    **(2 marks)**

> Be sure to show clearly that the overflow error is not part of the answer.

......................................................................................................................................

......................................................................................................................................

......................................................................................................................................

......................................................................................................................................

**Target grade 4-6**

**5** Describe one way an overflow error can be caused by shifting the 8-bit binary
pattern 1100 0011 left by one position.                                                                              **(2 marks)**

......................................................................................................................................

......................................................................................................................................

......................................................................................................................................

......................................................................................................................................

# Hexadecimal

**Target grade 1-3**

**1** (a) Explain why hexadecimal numbers are sometimes used to represent values stored in computers, even though computers do not use hexadecimal numbers.

**(2 marks)**

.................................................................................................................

.................................................................................................................

.................................................................................................................

.................................................................................................................

**Target grade 4-6**

(b) Convert the hexadecimal number A8 into an 8-bit binary number.

**(2 marks)**

> Remember to first convert the two digits into denary numbers if they are letters. They can then be converted into the two nibbles of the binary number.

.................................................................................................................

.................................................................................................................

.................................................................................................................

.................................................................................................................

.................................................................................................................

.................................................................................................................

(c) Convert the 8-bit binary numbers 1101 0101 and 1011 1101 into hexadecimal numbers.

> Remember to first convert the 8-bit number to nibbles and then convert each of these into a denary number.

**Target grade 4-6**

(i) 1101 0101

**(2 marks)**

.................................................................................................................

.................................................................................................................

.................................................................................................................

**Target grade 4-6**

(ii) 1011 1101

**(2 marks)**

.................................................................................................................

.................................................................................................................

.................................................................................................................

# Characters

**Target grade 1-3**

1  Define what is meant by the 'character set' of a computer.  **(2 marks)**

..................................................................................................................

..................................................................................................................

..................................................................................................................

..................................................................................................................

**Target grade 4-6**

2  Describe how ASCII is used to represent characters in a computer system.  **(2 marks)**

> You should say how many bits are used in the ASCII code. You should also say how many characters and actions can be represented.

..................................................................................................................

..................................................................................................................

..................................................................................................................

..................................................................................................................

**Target grade 1-3**

3  Here are two character strings.

| First | Second |
|-------|--------|
| Mary had a little lamb | У Мэри был маленький ягненок |

Describe **one** reason why the first string can be represented in ASCII but the second cannot be represented in ASCII.  **(2 marks)**

..................................................................................................................

..................................................................................................................

..................................................................................................................

..................................................................................................................

**Target grade 1-3**

4  The 7-bit ASCII code for the letter 'Q' is 81.
   Give the ASCII code for the letter 'H'.  **(1 mark)**

..................................................................................................................

..................................................................................................................

# Bitmap images

**Target grade 1-3**

1  This photograph is a bitmap image.

(a) State what is meant by the following terms.

The size of an image:

............................................................

............................................................

............................................................

............................................................

The resolution of an image:

**Figure 1**

............................................................................................................

............................................................................................................  **(2 marks)**

**Target grade 4-6**

(b) The number of colours represented in an image depends on the colour depth used.

Complete the table to show the number of colours that can be represented using the following colour depths.  **(3 marks)**

| Colour depth | Number of colours represented |
|:---:|:---:|
| 1 | |
| 3 | |
| 8 | |

**Target grade 4-6**

(c) The image in Figure 1 has the following properties:
width = 2000; height = 3000; colour depth = 24.

Construct an expression to calculate the size of the image file in mebibytes. You do not need to carry out the calculation.  **(3 marks)**

> It is important that you understand the rules of BIDMAS so that you do not make a mistake. If in any doubt, use brackets to show the order of operations.

............................................................................................................

............................................................................................................

............................................................................................................

............................................................................................................

# Analogue sound

**Target grade 1-3**

1  Sound can be represented digitally by taking samples of the original sound.

(a)  State what is meant by sample rate.  **(1 mark)**

.................................................................................................................

.................................................................................................................

**Target grade 1-3**

(b)  Describe the effect of increasing the sample rate.  **(2 marks)**

.................................................................................................................

.................................................................................................................

.................................................................................................................

.................................................................................................................

**Target grade 1-3**

2  (a)  Explain what is meant by the bit depth of a recording.  **(2 marks)**

.................................................................................................................

.................................................................................................................

.................................................................................................................

**Target grade 1-3**

(b)  State the effect of increasing the bit depth of a recording.  **(1 mark)**

.................................................................................................................

.................................................................................................................

.................................................................................................................

**Target grade 4-6**

3  The sample rate and bit depth affect the size of the file produced.
Name **two** other factors which will affect the size of the file.  **(2 marks)**

Factor 1 ..........................................................................................

Factor 2 ..........................................................................................

**Target grade 4-6**

4  Construct an expression to calculate the file size, in mebibytes, of a
100-second recording with a sample rate of 44.1 kHz if 16 bits are used
to encode each sample.  **(3 marks)**

> You should always show your working in questions involving calculations.
> You may get some credit for showing that you understand the method even
> if your final answer is wrong.

.................................................................................................................

.................................................................................................................

.................................................................................................................

# Limitations of binary representation of data

**Target grade 1-3**

1 Give all the distinct bit patterns that can be generated with three bits.

(2 marks)

.................................................................................................................

.................................................................................................................

.................................................................................................................

**Target grade 1-3**

2 State the formula used to determine the number of distinct binary patterns for a known number of bits (n).

(1 mark)

> When writing formulas as answers to questions, make sure your writing is clear. You can use brackets to make sure the order of the operation (BIDMAS) is very clear.

.................................................................................................................

.................................................................................................................

**Target grade 1-3**

3 Identify the number of bits used to represent characters in the ASCII character set.

(1 mark)

☐ **A** 10

☐ **B** 8

☐ **C** 7

☐ **D** 3

**Target grade 4-6**

4 Describe the reason 4 bits may be the preferred way to store colour depth in an image rather than 8 bits.

(2 marks)

.................................................................................................................

.................................................................................................................

.................................................................................................................

.................................................................................................................

**Target grade 4-6**

5 Explain **one** reason why the bit depth of an audio recording may be reduced.

(2 marks)

.................................................................................................................

.................................................................................................................

.................................................................................................................

.................................................................................................................

# Binary units of measurement

**1** Kibi and gibi are used as prefixes for the units of measurement relating to data storage. Identify the numeric base for these prefixes. **(1 mark)**

☐ **A** 8

☐ **B** 16

☐ **C** 10

☐ **D** 2

**2** Here are the units of measurement for data storage: bit, byte, gibibyte, kibibyte, mebibyte, nibble and tebibyte. Complete the table to put them in order from smallest to largest. One has been done for you. **(3 marks)**

| Order | Smallest | | | | | | Largest |
|-------|----------|--|--|--|--|--|---------|
| Unit  |          |  | byte |  |  |  |      |

**3** A file has a size of 72 000 000 000 bits.

Construct an expression to show this in gibibytes. **(4 marks)**

.................................................................................................................................

.................................................................................................................................

.................................................................................................................................

.................................................................................................................................

.................................................................................................................................

**4** An image file is 5312 pixels wide and 2988 pixels high. The colour depth is 16 bits.

Construct an expression to show the size of the file in mebibytes. **(4 marks)**

> In this question, you have to remember how to calculate the number of pixels in an image and what colour depth means. The formula for calculating the number of bits in an image is:
>
> (width in pixels) × (height in pixels) × (colour depth in bits).

.................................................................................................................................

.................................................................................................................................

.................................................................................................................................

.................................................................................................................................

.................................................................................................................................

# Data compression

**1** Leah is sending files to her brother Ollie while he is away on holiday by attaching them to emails. The files include images, music, and PDF and word-processed documents.

**Target grade 1-3**

(a)  Identify **two** advantages for Leah and Ollie of compressing the files. **(2 marks)**

1 ................................................................................................................................

...................................................................................................................................

2 ................................................................................................................................

...................................................................................................................................

**Target grade 1-3**

(b)  Two types of compression are lossless and lossy.
     Describe the difference between lossless and lossy compression. **(4 marks)**

...................................................................................................................................

...................................................................................................................................

...................................................................................................................................

...................................................................................................................................

...................................................................................................................................

...................................................................................................................................

...................................................................................................................................

...................................................................................................................................

**Target grade 4-6**

(c)  State which type of compression is appropriate for each of the following files that Leah sends and explain why it is appropriate. **(4 marks)**

(i)  **A PDF file of a novel.**

Type of compression ..................................................................................

Reason ........................................................................................................

...................................................................................................................................

...................................................................................................................................

(ii)  **Images of her trip to London.**

Type of compression ..................................................................................

Reason ........................................................................................................

...................................................................................................................................

...................................................................................................................................

# The stored program concept

**Target grade 1-3**

**1** Von Neumann developed the stored program concept.
State the **two** items he proposed to store in main memory. **(2 marks)**

1 ...........................................................................................................................

2 ...........................................................................................................................

**Target grade 1-3**

**2** List **two** hardware components with which the CPU works to execute
program instructions. **(2 marks)**

> This question is not asking about components within the CPU.

1 ...........................................................................................................................

2 ...........................................................................................................................

**Target grade 4-6**

**3** Explain **one** reason the memory in a computer is described as 'random access'. **(2 marks)**

...........................................................................................................................

...........................................................................................................................

...........................................................................................................................

...........................................................................................................................

**Target grade 1-3**

**4** Identify the part of the CPU that sends signals to other components. **(1 mark)**

☐ **A** Address bus

☐ **B** Arithmetic logic unit

☐ **C** Control unit

☐ **D** Register

# The central processing unit

 **Target grade 1-3**

1 This table provides information about the components of the CPU.
Complete the table by filling in the missing information.

**(4 marks)**

| Hardware component | Function |
|---|---|
| Control unit (CU) | |
| | Controls the rate at which program instructions are executed. |
| Arithmetic logic unit (ALU) | |
| | Provides direct-access storage for instructions, intermediate results and data within the CPU. |

**Target grade 4-6**

2 Here is a diagram of the inside of a computer.
Name the items labelled A, B, C, D and E.

**(5 marks)**

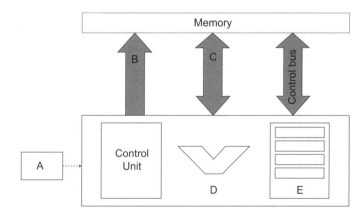

Only one of the three buses is unidirectional. The other two are bidirectional.

A ...................................................    D ...................................................

B ...................................................    E ...................................................

C ...................................................

**Target grade 4-6**

3 Explain how the speed of the clock affects the performance of the CPU.

**(2 marks)**

........................................................................................................................

........................................................................................................................

........................................................................................................................

........................................................................................................................

**35**

# The fetch-decode-execute cycle

**Target grade 1-3**

1  The CPU uses the fetch-decode-execute cycle to execute program instructions.

   (a)  The table below describes stages in the fetch-decode-execute cycle but they are not in order. Write the numbers 1–4 in the empty cells to show the correct order. **(2 marks)**

| Description | Order |
|---|---|
| The next instruction is sent from the RAM to the CPU. | |
| The instruction is carried out. | |
| The CU interprets the instruction. | |
| The CPU sends a signal to the RAM requesting the next instruction. | |

**Target grade 1-3**

   (b)  State the role of RAM in the fetch-decode-execute cycle. **(1 mark)**

   .................................................................................................................

   .................................................................................................................

**Target grade 1-3**

   (c)  Annotate the diagram to show the role of the CU and ALU in the fetch-decode-execute cycle. **(2 marks)**

| CU (control unit) | ALU (arithmetic logic unit) |
|---|---|
| The CU _____ the instructions. If a calculation is needed, the CU instructs the _____ . | _____ are carried out in the ALU. |

**Target grade 4-6**

2  Within the CPU are memory locations called **registers**.
   Describe their role in the fetch-decode-execute cycle. **(2 marks)**

   .................................................................................................................

   .................................................................................................................

   .................................................................................................................

   .................................................................................................................

**Target grade 4-6**

3  Describe the process that takes place when the program instruction stored in memory location 0101 1101 is read into the CPU. **(3 marks)**

   .................................................................................................................

   .................................................................................................................

   .................................................................................................................

   .................................................................................................................

   .................................................................................................................

# The need for secondary storage

**Target grade 1-3**

1   Complete the table below by putting a tick in the column that matches the description.   **(3 marks)**

| Description | Primary storage | Secondary storage |
|---|---|---|
| Non-volatile | | |
| Directly accessible by the CPU | | |
| Storage over 1 TiB | | |

**Target grade 4-6**

2   Describe how memory and secondary storage work together to run an application stored in a file.   **(3 marks)**

> There are three marks for this question, so you must make three distinct points.

.................................................................................................................................

.................................................................................................................................

.................................................................................................................................

.................................................................................................................................

.................................................................................................................................

.................................................................................................................................

**Target grade 1-3**

3   Explain how secondary storage helps computers to perform a variety of tasks.   **(2 marks)**

.................................................................................................................................

.................................................................................................................................

.................................................................................................................................

.................................................................................................................................

# Types of secondary storage

**Target grade 1-3**

1 Complete the table by naming the types of secondary storage described in each row. **(3 marks)**

> It is a category of storage that is needed, not a type of storage device.
> Responses such as 'hard disc', 'CD' or 'flash drive' will not gain any mark.

| Type of secondary storage | Description |
|---|---|
| | Uses metal platters coated in iron oxide. The platters rotate at high speed. |
| | Small pits are burned in patterns onto a flat surface. A laser can be used to interpret light reflected from the flat or pitted surface. |
| | No moving parts; data is stored as an electrical charge. |

**Target grade 4-6**

2 Give **two** reasons a laptop with a solid-state drive is preferable to one with a magnetic hard drive. **(2 marks)**

1 ........................................................................................................

........................................................................................................

2 ........................................................................................................

........................................................................................................

**Target grade 4-6**

3 (a) Describe how data is stored on a DVD disk. **(3 marks)**

........................................................................................................

........................................................................................................

........................................................................................................

........................................................................................................

........................................................................................................

**Target grade 4-6**

(b) A dance school makes video recordings of its pupils' performances.
Give **two** features of optical storage that make it suitable for distributing the videos to parents. **(2 marks)**

1 ........................................................................................................

........................................................................................................

2 ........................................................................................................

........................................................................................................

# Embedded systems

**Target grade 1-3**

**1** Define what is meant by an embedded system.

(1 mark)

..................................................................................................................

..................................................................................................................

**Target grade 4-6**

**2** Give **three** components of an embedded system.

(3 marks)

1 ...............................................................................................................

..................................................................................................................

2 ...............................................................................................................

..................................................................................................................

3 ...............................................................................................................

..................................................................................................................

**Target grade 4-6**

**3** A smart t-shirt streams real-time work-out data, such as heart rate and lung function, to the wearer's phone.

Explain how the embedded system in the t-shirt can do this.

(2 marks)

> You are not expected to go into depth – focus on how the data will be captured and transferred from the t-shirt to the wearer's phone.

..................................................................................................................

..................................................................................................................

..................................................................................................................

..................................................................................................................

# Operating system 1

**Target grade 1-3**

**1** State the purpose of a scheduling algorithm.                                                    **(1 mark)**

> Do not get scheduling and paging muddled up – one is to do with the CPU
> and the other with memory usage.

.................................................................................................................................

.................................................................................................................................

**Target grade 4-6**

**2** Describe how an active process differs from an inactive process.                           **(2 marks)**

.................................................................................................................................

.................................................................................................................................

.................................................................................................................................

.................................................................................................................................

**Target grade 1-3**

**3** Describe how virtual memory works.                                                            **(3 marks)**

> Use the number of marks as a guide for how much to write.

.................................................................................................................................

.................................................................................................................................

.................................................................................................................................

.................................................................................................................................

.................................................................................................................................

.................................................................................................................................

**Target grade 4-6**

**4** State the purpose of a paging algorithm.                                                      **(1 mark)**

.................................................................................................................................

.................................................................................................................................

# Operating system 2

Target grade 1-3

**1** State the function of a device driver.

**(1 mark)**

.................................................................................................

.................................................................................................

Target grade 4-6

**2** Erik and Lola work for a major international aircraft manufacturer. Erik works in management and deals with corporate clients. Lola is an electrical engineer. She is part of the team responsible for assembling aircraft wings.

(a) Explain the type of access that Lola should have to the company's design drawings of aircraft wings.

**(2 marks)**

> Use the word 'because' to justify the choice of access you choose.

.................................................................................................

.................................................................................................

.................................................................................................

.................................................................................................

Target grade 4-6

(b) Explain the type of access that Erik should have to email software.

**(2 marks)**

.................................................................................................

.................................................................................................

.................................................................................................

.................................................................................................

Target grade 4-6

(c) Explain the type of access that Lola should have to an article she has written for the company's newsletter.

**(2 marks)**

.................................................................................................

.................................................................................................

.................................................................................................

.................................................................................................

Had a go ☐   Nearly there ☐   Nailed it! ☐

# Utility software

**1** Stephen's computer is running slowly and he thinks it is because his hard disk drive is fragmented.

**Target grade 1-3**

(a) State what is meant by 'fragmented'. **(1 mark)**

.................................................................................................................

.................................................................................................................

**Target grade 4-6**

(b) Explain how defragmentation software will help to make the computer run more quickly. **(2 marks)**

.................................................................................................................

.................................................................................................................

.................................................................................................................

.................................................................................................................

(c) Stephen is advised to use data compression software to create more space on his hard disk drive.

**Target grade 1-3**

   (i) Give another instance when Stephen should use compression software. **(1 mark)**

.................................................................................................................

.................................................................................................................

**Target grade 4-6**

   (ii) Describe the difference between lossless and lossy compression. **(2 marks)**

.................................................................................................................

.................................................................................................................

.................................................................................................................

.................................................................................................................

**Target grade 4-6**

**2** Anti-malware software is a type of utility software.

Describe **two** methods that this software uses to identify malware. **(4 marks)**

.................................................................................................................

.................................................................................................................

.................................................................................................................

.................................................................................................................

.................................................................................................................

.................................................................................................................

.................................................................................................................

.................................................................................................................

# Robust software

**Target grade 1-3**

**1** Give **two** features of robust software.

**(2 marks)**

1 ...........................................................................................................................

...........................................................................................................................

2 ...........................................................................................................................

...........................................................................................................................

**Target grade 4-6**

**2** Explain **one** way in which conducting regular code reviews helps ensure that software is robust.

**(2 marks)**

...........................................................................................................................

...........................................................................................................................

...........................................................................................................................

...........................................................................................................................

**Target grade 4-6**

**3** Explain **one** way in which keeping an audit trail helps developers to remedy an error they have identified in a piece of code.

**(2 marks)**

> When answering an explain question, think about using 'because' or phrases such as 'this means' and 'this is why' to expand on the point you have made.

...........................................................................................................................

...........................................................................................................................

...........................................................................................................................

...........................................................................................................................

# Programming languages

**Target grade 1-3**

**1** Give **three** features of a 'high-level language'. **(3 marks)**

1 ................................................................................................................................

................................................................................................................................

2 ................................................................................................................................

................................................................................................................................

3 ................................................................................................................................

................................................................................................................................

**Target grade 4-6**

**2** Describe **one** way in which assembly language differs from machine code. **(2 marks)**

................................................................................................................................

................................................................................................................................

................................................................................................................................

................................................................................................................................

**Target grade 7-9**

**3** One benefit of using a high-level language to write software is that the details of a computer's architecture are abstracted away, enabling the programmer to focus on the program logic.

Explain **one** drawback of this approach. **(3 marks)**

> Use the number of marks allocated to a question as a guide for how many distinct points you should make. In this case it is three. At least one of these points must provide your justification for your answer, because the command word is 'explain'.

................................................................................................................................

................................................................................................................................

................................................................................................................................

................................................................................................................................

................................................................................................................................

................................................................................................................................

# Interpreters and compilers

**Target grade 1-3**

1 Computers can only execute instructions written in machine code.

   (a) State the name of the software used to translate a program written in assembly language into machine code. **(1 mark)**

   .......................................................................................................................................

**Target grade 4-6**

   (b) Describe how a compiler differs from an interpreter in the way it translates code. **(2 marks)**

   .......................................................................................................................................

   .......................................................................................................................................

   .......................................................................................................................................

   .......................................................................................................................................

**Target grade 4-6**

2 A programmer is writing software for a new set-top receiver for satellite TV. Describe **one** reason the programmer should use a compiler instead of an interpreter to translate the code. **(2 marks)**

   .......................................................................................................................................

   .......................................................................................................................................

   .......................................................................................................................................

   .......................................................................................................................................

**Target grade 7-9**

3 Evie wants to learn to program. Discuss the suitability of compiled and interpreted programming languages for Evie. **(6 marks)**

   .......................................................................................................................................

   .......................................................................................................................................

   .......................................................................................................................................

   .......................................................................................................................................

   .......................................................................................................................................

   .......................................................................................................................................

   .......................................................................................................................................

   .......................................................................................................................................

   .......................................................................................................................................

   .......................................................................................................................................

   .......................................................................................................................................

# Networks

**Target grade 1-3**

**1** State **two** reasons for connecting computers in a network. **(2 marks)**

1 .................................................................................................................

.................................................................................................................

2 .................................................................................................................

.................................................................................................................

**2** Two types of network are a LAN (local area network) and a WAN (wide area network).

> You are being asked to 'describe' the characteristics of a LAN and a WAN so do not just state what each one is. You must describe some of the features of each one. Use the number of marks as a guide for the number of points you need to make.

**Target grade 4-6**

(a) Describe the characteristics of a LAN. **(3 marks)**

.................................................................................................................

.................................................................................................................

.................................................................................................................

.................................................................................................................

**Target grade 4-6**

(b) Describe the characteristics of a WAN. **(3 marks)**

.................................................................................................................

.................................................................................................................

.................................................................................................................

.................................................................................................................

**Target grade 4-6**

**3** An intruder detection system is installed in an office. Motion sensors throughout the building continually send data to a monitoring device on the ground floor. When an intruder is detected, the monitoring device contacts the police and switches on a siren. The intruder detection system uses both a LAN and a WAN. Identify which aspects of the system use a LAN and which use the WAN. **(3 marks)**

.................................................................................................................

.................................................................................................................

.................................................................................................................

.................................................................................................................

# The internet

**Target grade 1-3**

**1** Give **one** reason an internet-connected device needs an IP address.  **(1 mark)**

.........................................................................................................................................

.........................................................................................................................................

**Target grade 1-3**

**2** (a)  Define what is meant by the term 'URL'.  **(2 marks)**

.........................................................................................................................................

.........................................................................................................................................

.........................................................................................................................................

.........................................................................................................................................

**Target grade 4-6**

(b)  Explain **one** reason URLs rather than IP addresses are used to locate a resource server on the internet.  **(3 marks)**

.........................................................................................................................................

.........................................................................................................................................

.........................................................................................................................................

.........................................................................................................................................

.........................................................................................................................................

.........................................................................................................................................

**Target grade 4-6**

**3** A user types the URL of a web page into their browser's address bar.

Describe the role of a DNS server in finding the location of the web page on the internet.  **(2 marks)**

.........................................................................................................................................

.........................................................................................................................................

.........................................................................................................................................

.........................................................................................................................................

# Packet switching

**Target grade 1-3**

**1** Data is transmitted across the internet in packets.

(a) Define what is meant by a 'data packet'. **(2 marks)**

.................................................................................................................

.................................................................................................................

.................................................................................................................

.................................................................................................................

**Target grade 1-3**

(b) Name **three** pieces of information included in a packet header. **(3 marks)**

1 ..............................................................................................................

.................................................................................................................

2 ..............................................................................................................

.................................................................................................................

3 ..............................................................................................................

.................................................................................................................

**Target grade 4-6**

(c) Describe how packets are transmitted across the internet. **(4 marks)**

> Routers play an important part in data transmission across the internet, so try to include several different aspects of their role in your answer.

.................................................................................................................

.................................................................................................................

.................................................................................................................

.................................................................................................................

.................................................................................................................

.................................................................................................................

.................................................................................................................

# Wired versus wireless

**1** Bandwidth and latency are two important factors that affect the performance of networks.

**Target grade 1-3**

(a) Define the term 'bandwidth'. **(1 mark)**

.................................................................................................................................

.................................................................................................................................

**Target grade 1-3**

(b) Define the term 'latency'. **(1 mark)**

.................................................................................................................................

.................................................................................................................................

**2** The Smarts Leisure Group is opening a new regional office.

The company has chosen wireless rather than wired connectivity for its new building.

**Target grade 4-6**

(a) Give **two** reasons the company might prefer wireless connectivity. **(2 marks)**

1 ..............................................................................................................................

.................................................................................................................................

2 ..............................................................................................................................

.................................................................................................................................

**Target grade 4-6**

(b) The company stores its customers' financial details on a network-connected computer.

Explain **one** reason wired networks are more secure than wireless networks. **(2 marks)**

> Part (a) requires you to 'give a reason', whereas in part (b) you are asked to 'explain a reason', so you need to give a fuller answer consisting of two linked statements.

.................................................................................................................................

.................................................................................................................................

.................................................................................................................................

.................................................................................................................................

# Connectivity on a LAN

**Target grade 1-3**

1  Devices on a LAN can be connected using a wired or wireless transmission medium.

(a)  State what is meant by the term 'transmission medium'.  **(1 mark)**

...................................................................................................................................

...................................................................................................................................

**Target grade 1-3**

(b)  The type of transmission medium used impacts on a network's performance.

Give **one** reason why wireless networks generally have higher latency than wired networks.  **(1 mark)**

> Latency is the time between the data being transmitted and the moment it reaches its destination.

...................................................................................................................................

...................................................................................................................................

**Target grade 4-6**

(c)  The manufacturer of a network attached storage (NAS) drive recommends that it is connected to the router via a wired Ethernet connection.

Explain **one** reason why the NAS on a home network should be physically connected by a cable to the router.  **(2 marks)**

...................................................................................................................................

...................................................................................................................................

...................................................................................................................................

...................................................................................................................................

**Target grade 7-9**

2  NFC is a wireless transmission method used in contactless payment applications.

Describe how an NFC contactless payment system works.  **(3 marks)**

...................................................................................................................................

...................................................................................................................................

...................................................................................................................................

...................................................................................................................................

...................................................................................................................................

...................................................................................................................................

# Network speeds

**Target grade 1-3**

**1** State the unit of measurement used for the data transfer rate of a network. **(1 mark)**

......................................................................................................................................

**Target grade 7-9**

**2** Construct an expression to calculate the transmission rate in Kbps required to transmit a 1.2 GiB file in 15 minutes. You do not need to do the calculation. **(4 marks)**

> The marks are awarded for creating a mathematical expression – a combination of values, variables and operators – that evaluates to a single value. Do not waste time doing the calculation. You will not get any marks for giving the answer.

......................................................................................................................................

......................................................................................................................................

......................................................................................................................................

......................................................................................................................................

**Target grade 7-9**

**3** Construct an expression to show how many seconds it will take to transmit 286 MiB of data across a network with a data transmission speed of 3.2 Gbps. You do not need to do the calculation. **(3 marks)**

> Make sure that you convert all values so that they have common units (i.e. they are all expressed using the lowest common unit). In this case, it is the size of the file in bits that is divided by the speed in bits per second.

......................................................................................................................................

......................................................................................................................................

......................................................................................................................................

......................................................................................................................................

**Target grade 7-9**

**4** Construct an expression to calculate the size of a file (in mebibytes) that takes 5 minutes to transmit across a network that has a transmission rate of 6.8 Gbps. You do not need to do the calculation. **(4 marks)**

......................................................................................................................................

......................................................................................................................................

......................................................................................................................................

......................................................................................................................................

# Network protocols

**Target grade 1-3**

1  Explain **one** reason network protocols are needed.  **(2 marks)**

.................................................................................................................

.................................................................................................................

.................................................................................................................

.................................................................................................................

**Target grade 4-6**

2  Anja is setting up a website so that she can move her skincare business online.
Explain **one** reason her website should use HTTPS rather than HTTP.  **(3 marks)**

> Use the marks allocated to an 'explain' question as a guide to how many
> distinct points you should make in your response. In this case the question
> describes a scenario, so make sure your response takes this into account.
> A generic answer will not suffice.

.................................................................................................................

.................................................................................................................

.................................................................................................................

.................................................................................................................

.................................................................................................................

.................................................................................................................

**Target grade 4-6**

3  Jayden sometimes accesses his email on his phone and sometimes on his laptop.
Describe **one** reason the IMAP protocol is more suitable for Jayden to use than
the POP3 protocol.  **(2 marks)**

.................................................................................................................

.................................................................................................................

.................................................................................................................

.................................................................................................................

# The TCP/IP model

**Target grade 1-3**

**1** Define what is meant by the term 'protocol stack'.    **(1 mark)**

> Do not simply repeat the words given in the question in your response.
> Simply writing 'A stack of protocols' will not earn you the mark.

.......................................................................................................................

.......................................................................................................................

**2** One or more protocols operate at each layer of the TCP/IP stack.

**Target grade 1-3**

    (a)  Name **two** protocols that operate at the Application layer.    **(2 marks)**

    1 .................................................................................................................

    2 .................................................................................................................

**Target grade 1-3**

    (b)  Name **two** protocols that operate at the Link layer.    **(2 marks)**

    1 .................................................................................................................

    2 .................................................................................................................

**3** The TCP/IP stack is named after two of the protocols in the stack: TCP and IP.

**Target grade 4-6**

    (a)  Describe the role of TCP in preparing outgoing data for transmission across the internet.    **(3 marks)**

.......................................................................................................................

.......................................................................................................................

.......................................................................................................................

.......................................................................................................................

.......................................................................................................................

.......................................................................................................................

**Target grade 4-6**

    (b)  Describe the role of IP in preparing outgoing data for transmission across the internet.    **(2 marks)**

.......................................................................................................................

.......................................................................................................................

.......................................................................................................................

.......................................................................................................................

# Network topologies

**Target grade 1-3**

1   Define what is meant by a 'network topology'.      **(1 mark)**

.............................................................................................................................

.............................................................................................................................

**Target grade 1-3**

2   Complete this table by matching each characteristic to a topology.      **(3 marks)**

| Characteristic | Bus | Star | Mesh |
|---|---|---|---|
| Each device is connected to a central routing device | | | |
| Each device has a dedicated connection to one or more devices | | | |
| Each device is connected to a central cable | | | |

**Target grade 4-6**

3   One feature of fully-connected mesh networks is that they are self-healing. Describe how this is achieved.      **(2 marks)**

> Self-healing means that the network will carry on operating even if a node or connection fails. There is no need to define the term 'self-healing' in your answer. In your response focus on how self-healing is achieved.

.............................................................................................................................

.............................................................................................................................

.............................................................................................................................

.............................................................................................................................

**Target grade 4-6**

4   Describe **one** reason the performance of a bus network degrades as more devices are added to it.      **(3 marks)**

.............................................................................................................................

.............................................................................................................................

.............................................................................................................................

.............................................................................................................................

.............................................................................................................................

.............................................................................................................................

# Network security

1 A company is concerned about the security of its network. It employs an ethical hacker to carry out penetration testing.

**Target grade 1-3**

(a) Define what is meant by the term 'ethical hacker'. **(1 mark)**

.......................................................................................................................

.......................................................................................................................

**Target grade 1-3**

(b) Describe what is meant by the term 'penetration testing' when applied to networks. **(2 marks)**

.......................................................................................................................

.......................................................................................................................

**Target grade 7-9**

2 Discuss the importance of network security for organisations. **(6 marks)**

> You might find it useful to use headings to structure your answer.
> You could start by discussing what network security entails and then go on to consider the potential impacts of a security breach (e.g. business disruption, financial loss, reputational damage, legal implications, etc.).

.......................................................................................................................

.......................................................................................................................

.......................................................................................................................

.......................................................................................................................

.......................................................................................................................

.......................................................................................................................

.......................................................................................................................

.......................................................................................................................

.......................................................................................................................

.......................................................................................................................

.......................................................................................................................

.......................................................................................................................

# Protecting networks

1 A company's network server is installed in a dedicated room. Authorised users are issued with a 4-digit PIN, which they must enter into a keypad to gain access to the room.

**Target grade 1-3**

(a) List **three** other physical security measures the company could take to control access to the server room. **(3 marks)**

1 ..................................................................................................................

..................................................................................................................

2 ..................................................................................................................

..................................................................................................................

3 ..................................................................................................................

..................................................................................................................

(b) The company wants to replace keypad authentication with some form of biometric authentication.

**Target grade 1-3**

(i) Give **two** types of biometric authentication that are in common use. **(2 marks)**

1 ..............................................................................................................

2 ..............................................................................................................

**Target grade 4-6**

(ii) Describe **one** advantage of using a biometric access system rather than a keypad. **(2 marks)**

..................................................................................................................

..................................................................................................................

..................................................................................................................

..................................................................................................................

**Target grade 4-6**

(c) The company employs a number of freelance consultants to run staff training courses. Consultants log on to the company's network to look up information about the employees booked onto their courses. The company's human resource department staff are the only people who are allowed to amend an employee's record.

Describe **one** way file permissions can be used to allow this to happen so that security is maintained. **(4 marks)**

..................................................................................................................

..................................................................................................................

..................................................................................................................

..................................................................................................................

..................................................................................................................

..................................................................................................................

# Environmental issues 1

**Target grade 1-3**

1   Describe **one** way in which the manufacture of digital devices harms the environment.

(2 marks)

.............................................................................................

.............................................................................................

.............................................................................................

.............................................................................................

.............................................................................................

.............................................................................................

**Target grade 4-6**

2   Explain **two** ways the improper disposal of digital devices is harmful to the environment.

(4 marks)

> The question asks for 'two ways', so treat it as two 'explain' questions, each worth two marks. For each one, make a statement and then use 'because', 'therefore', 'and so', etc. to link to an explanation.

1 .........................................................................................

.............................................................................................

.............................................................................................

.............................................................................................

2 .........................................................................................

.............................................................................................

.............................................................................................

.............................................................................................

**Target grade 1-3**

3   List **three** ways responsible recycling can reduce the environmental damage caused by e-waste.

(3 marks)

1 .........................................................................................

.............................................................................................

2 .........................................................................................

.............................................................................................

3 .........................................................................................

.............................................................................................

# Environmental issues 2

Target grade 1-3

1   Explain **one** way in which the use of digital technologies is helping the environment.

**(2 marks)**

.................................................................................................................................

.................................................................................................................................

.................................................................................................................................

.................................................................................................................................

2   Niamh has bought a new laptop. She does not want her old one to become e-waste and be dumped in a landfill.

Target grade 1-3

(a)   Describe **one** environmentally friendly way in which Niamh can dispose of her old laptop.

**(2 marks)**

> There is no need to give a justification or a reason when the command word is 'describe', but you should try to make two linked statements. In this case, choose an action that Niamh can take and then say something pertinent about it.

.................................................................................................................................

.................................................................................................................................

.................................................................................................................................

.................................................................................................................................

Target grade 1-3

(b)   Responsible recycling is one way of reducing the negative environmental impact of digital devices.

State **three other** ways to reduce the negative impact of digital devices on the environment.

**(3 marks)**

1 ...........................................................................................................................

.................................................................................................................................

2 ...........................................................................................................................

.................................................................................................................................

3 ...........................................................................................................................

.................................................................................................................................

# Personal data

**Target grade 1-3**

**1** Define what is meant by 'personal data'.     **(1 mark)**

.................................................................................................................................

.................................................................................................................................

**Target grade 4-6**

**2** Explain why retailers collect data about their customers.     **(3 marks)**

.................................................................................................................................

.................................................................................................................................

.................................................................................................................................

.................................................................................................................................

.................................................................................................................................

.................................................................................................................................

**Target grade 4-6**

**3** Sarah has location tracking on her mobile phone.
Give **two** ways in which location tracking has an impact on Sarah's privacy.     **(2 marks)**

1 ............................................................................................................................

.................................................................................................................................

2 ............................................................................................................................

.................................................................................................................................

**Target grade 4-6**

**4** Explain **one** ethical concern associated with the use of Internet of Things (IoT) devices in the home.     **(2 marks)**

.................................................................................................................................

.................................................................................................................................

.................................................................................................................................

.................................................................................................................................

# Legislation

**1** A school uses an information management system to store details of students, parents and staff.

Target grade **1-3**

(a) State the legislation which governs how the school can store and use these details. **(1 mark)**

..................................................................................................................

..................................................................................................................

Target grade **4-6**

(b) List **three** rights that people (data subjects) have regarding the data that is stored about them. **(3 marks)**

1 ...............................................................................................................

2 ...............................................................................................................

3 ...............................................................................................................

Target grade **4-6**

(c) List **three** responsibilities the school has regarding the collection and storage of data. **(3 marks)**

1 ...............................................................................................................

2 ...............................................................................................................

3 ...............................................................................................................

Target grade **4-6**

**2** The Computer Misuse Act 1990 identifies three types of offences:

A    unauthorised access to computer material

B    unauthorised access with intent to commit further offences

C    unauthorised access with intent to impair the running of a computer or to damage or destroy data

Complete the table below by entering A, B or C in the box beside each action to state the type of offence being commited. **(5 marks)**

| Action | Type of offence |
|---|---|
| A student accesses another student's email account without permission. | |
| A black-hat hacker exploits a security loophole in the school's network to launch a ransomware attack. | |
| A student accesses their parents' stored credit card numbers and security codes in order to buy goods online without their permission. | |
| A student guesses the login names and passwords of other students and logs into their accounts to read their emails. | |
| A computer science student successfully guesses the network manager's password. He uses it to gain access to the school's data management system and deletes all the staff records. | |

# Artificial intelligence (AI)

**Target grade 1-3**

**1** Define what is meant by 'artificial intelligence'. **(1 mark)**

......................................................................................................................

......................................................................................................................

**Target grade 4-6**

**2** Explain **one** way a machine-learning system can produce biased results. **(2 marks)**

......................................................................................................................

......................................................................................................................

......................................................................................................................

......................................................................................................................

**Target grade 7-9**

**3** Explain **one** reason it is difficult to establish accountability for any harm that has been caused by a machine-learning system. **(2 marks)**

> Think about how machine-learning algorithms differ from traditional algorithms.

......................................................................................................................

......................................................................................................................

......................................................................................................................

......................................................................................................................

**Target grade 7-9**

**4** Digital assistants, such as Apple's Siri and Google's Alexa, are categorised as 'narrow AI'.

Describe what is meant by the term 'narrow AI'. **(2 marks)**

......................................................................................................................

......................................................................................................................

......................................................................................................................

......................................................................................................................

......................................................................................................................

......................................................................................................................

# Protecting intellectual property 1

**Target grade 1-3**

1 Describe what is meant by 'intellectual property'. **(1 mark)**

........................................................................................................................

........................................................................................................................

**Target grade 4-6**

2 Explain how a copyright differs from a patent. **(4 marks)**

> When you see the 'explain' command word along with a word like 'differs',
> you are being asked to compare two things. In this case, start by explaining
> how copyright protects intellectual property and then explain how a
> patent does this differently. Try to link the two parts of your response with
> 'whereas' or 'on the other hand'.

........................................................................................................................

........................................................................................................................

........................................................................................................................

........................................................................................................................

........................................................................................................................

........................................................................................................................

........................................................................................................................

........................................................................................................................

**Target grade 4-6**

3 Dave wants to permit other people to use the graphics images he has produced.
Explain **one** reason a creative commons licence is suitable for this purpose. **(2 marks)**

........................................................................................................................

........................................................................................................................

........................................................................................................................

........................................................................................................................

**Target grade 4-6**

4 A company has registered its logo as a trademark.
Explain **one** reason it may decide to take legal action against someone who uses
the logo without permission. **(2 marks)**

........................................................................................................................

........................................................................................................................

........................................................................................................................

........................................................................................................................

# Protecting intellectual property 2

**1** Microsoft Office, as an example, is proprietary software.

**Target grade 1-3**

(a) Define what is meant by 'proprietary software'.    **(2 marks)**

...........................................................................................................................

...........................................................................................................................

...........................................................................................................................

...........................................................................................................................

**Target grade 4-6**

(b) The source code of proprietary software is kept secret.

Explain **one** reason some software developers choose to keep their source code secret.    **(2 marks)**

...........................................................................................................................

...........................................................................................................................

...........................................................................................................................

...........................................................................................................................

**Target grade 4-6**

(c) Ibrahim wants to buy a computer-aided design (CAD) package for his business. He has no experience of using CAD.

Explain **one** reason a proprietary CAD software package would be better for Ibrahim than one based on open-source software.    **(2 marks)**

> Make sure your response takes the context into account. Ibrahim is an inexperienced user with a business to run. He is unlikely to have a great deal of time to teach himself how to use any software he buys.

...........................................................................................................................

...........................................................................................................................

...........................................................................................................................

...........................................................................................................................

# Threats to digital systems 1

**Target grade 1-3**

1 Hackers use malware to carry out cybercrime.

(a) Describe what is meant by the term 'malware'.          **(3 marks)**

..................................................................................................................

..................................................................................................................

..................................................................................................................

..................................................................................................................

..................................................................................................................

..................................................................................................................

**Target grade 4-6**

(b) Worms, viruses and Trojans are all varieties of malware.

Complete the table by placing a tick in the appropriate column(s) beside each characteristic.          **(4 marks)**

| Characteristic | Virus | Worm | Trojan |
|---|---|---|---|
| Self-replicates | | | |
| Human action required to spread | | | |

**Target grade 4-6**

2 Describe **one** way a hacker can gain backdoor access into a computer system.          **(4 marks)**

> Think about the tactics a hacker could employ to get malware downloaded.
> What type of malware would give them access to a computer system?
> How would it work? What would it give them access to?

..................................................................................................................

..................................................................................................................

..................................................................................................................

..................................................................................................................

..................................................................................................................

..................................................................................................................

..................................................................................................................

..................................................................................................................

# Threats to digital systems 2

**Target grade 1-3**

1  Hackers use technical vulnerabilities to attack systems.

(a)  State what is meant by the term 'technical vulnerability'.  **(1 mark)**

....................................................................................................................

....................................................................................................................

**Target grade 1-3**

(b)  One technical vulnerability is created by out-of-date anti-malware.
Describe **one** other technical vulnerability that hackers look out for.  **(2 marks)**

....................................................................................................................

....................................................................................................................

....................................................................................................................

....................................................................................................................

**Target grade 4-6**

(c)  Give **one** reason why it is important for an organisation to keep the
operating system software installed on its company laptops up to date.  **(1 mark)**

....................................................................................................................

....................................................................................................................

**Target grade 7-9**

2  Explain how hackers use port scanning to help them identify possible
attack targets.  **(2 marks)**

> Port scanning is a reconnaissance tool used by hackers to obtain
> information. In your answer, you should say what kind of information is
> obtained by port scanning and how it is used to plan a cyberattack.

....................................................................................................................

....................................................................................................................

....................................................................................................................

....................................................................................................................

Had a go ☐   Nearly there ☐   Nailed it! ☐

# Threats to digital systems 3

**Target grade 1-3**

**1** Describe what is meant by 'social engineering'.                                          **(2 marks)**

.......................................................................................................................................

.......................................................................................................................................

.......................................................................................................................................

**2** 'Pretexting' and 'quid pro quo' are two techniques used in social engineering attacks.

**Target grade 4-6**

(a) Describe a pretexting attack.                                                               **(4 marks)**

> There are four marks for this question, so you need to produce a detailed description: Who does the attacker pretend to be? What is their objective? What tactics do they use to con their victims?

.......................................................................................................................................

.......................................................................................................................................

.......................................................................................................................................

.......................................................................................................................................

.......................................................................................................................................

**Target grade 4-6**

(b) Describe a quid pro quo attack.                                                            **(4 marks)**

.......................................................................................................................................

.......................................................................................................................................

.......................................................................................................................................

.......................................................................................................................................

**Target grade 7-9**

**3** Explain **one** reason social engineering is regarded as a greater threat to digital systems than technical vulnerabilities.                                               **(2 marks)**

.......................................................................................................................................

.......................................................................................................................................

.......................................................................................................................................

.......................................................................................................................................

# Protecting digital systems 1

**Target grade 1-3**

**1** Give **one** reason sensitive data should be encrypted.                                    **(1 mark)**

.......................................................................................................

.......................................................................................................

**Target grade 1-3**

**2** Describe how symmetric encryption works.                                    **(2 marks)**

.......................................................................................................

.......................................................................................................

.......................................................................................................

.......................................................................................................

**3** Every digital device should have up-to-date anti-malware software installed.

**Target grade 4-6**

(a) Describe the function of the signature library in anti-malware software.                                    **(3 marks)**

.......................................................................................................

.......................................................................................................

.......................................................................................................

.......................................................................................................

.......................................................................................................

.......................................................................................................

**Target grade 7-9**

(b) Describe why some anti-malware software uses both signature-based and behaviour-based methods to detect viruses.                                    **(3 marks)**

> You will get marks for saying which viruses will be picked up by the signature-based method and which will not. Then explain how the behaviour-based method addresses the shortfall.

.......................................................................................................

.......................................................................................................

.......................................................................................................

.......................................................................................................

.......................................................................................................

.......................................................................................................

# Protecting digital systems 2

**1** All companies should have an acceptable use policy (AUP).

**Target grade 1-3**

(a) Describe the purpose of an AUP.

**(2 marks)**

> Be careful. You are not being asked to say what an AUP is, but what it is used for. There are two marks, so you need to describe two uses in your answer.

..............................................................................................................

..............................................................................................................

..............................................................................................................

..............................................................................................................

**Target grade 7-9**

(b) Explain **one** reason employees should be required to sign a copy of their company's AUP.

**(2 marks)**

..............................................................................................................

..............................................................................................................

..............................................................................................................

..............................................................................................................

**Target grade 4-6**

**2** Describe **one** way a backup and recovery procedure will help an organisation if there is a fire in its server room.

**(2 marks)**

..............................................................................................................

..............................................................................................................

..............................................................................................................

..............................................................................................................

# Decomposition and abstraction

**Target grade 1-3**

1  A program is required to find out if a person is too young, too old or the correct age to enter school as a student. The minimum age to enter school is 3 years old. The maximum age to enter school is 19 years.

> This question requires you to make some decisions. Start by identifying inputs, processes and outputs. Inputs and outputs must be fit for purpose and suitable for your audience. Use comments to express your decomposition and abstraction logic in your code.

Open file **69 Decomposition and abstraction Q1 Student.py**

Amend the code to:

- Accept the user's name.
- Accept the user's age.
- Determine the user's status.
- Display messages based on the user's status.
- Display a goodbye message on exit.

Do **not** add any additional functionality.

Save your amended code file as **69 Decomposition and abstraction Q1 Finished.py**

**(7 marks)**

**Target grade 7-9**

2  The stopping distance for a vehicle varies with its speed. Another factor that affects stopping distance is the thinking time the driver needs before pressing the brake pedal.

> Ensure your design is suitable to solve the problem and that your code works for anticipated inputs.

The formula to calculate the thinking time is:

$d = v \times t$

- $d$ is the thinking distance
- $v$ is the speed of the vehicle
- $t$ is the reaction time of the driver.

For example, a car travels at 8.9 meters per second. The driver has a reaction time of 0.7 seconds. The calculation to give a value for thinking time is $8.9 \times 0.7 = 6.23$.

Speeds vary from 2.2 m/s to 35.7 m/s. Reaction times vary from 0.15 to 0.80 seconds.

Open file **69 Decomposition and abstraction Q2 Student.py**

Write a program to meet these requirements:

- Accept user input.
- Calculate thinking distance.
- Display program output.

Save your amended code file as **69 Decomposition and abstraction Q2 Finished.py**

**(15 marks)**

# Read, analyse and refine programs

1 A program is needed to track the results from a local election. The data available includes the candidates' names, the number of votes they received and the percentage of the vote they got.

> This type of question asks you to start with some existing code and change it to meet some specific requirements. This question states that percentages should be reported to one decimal place. You will need to refine the code to make that happen.

The output of the program is shown here.

```
Candidate    Votes    Percent
- - - - - - - - - - - - - - - - - - - - - - - - - - -
Mattson       686      22.9
Blair         380      12.7
Leonhardt    1051      35.0
Miller        406      13.5
Rowan         477      15.9
:= = = = = = = = = = = = = = = = = = = = = = = = = =:
Total        3000     100.0
```

Open file **70 Read, analyse and refine programs Student.py**

Amend the code to meet these requirements:

- Align column headings and column contents.
- Display a separator line after column headings.
- Calculate the correct total votes.
- Format all the percentages to one decimal place.
- Add a comment to identify the line that holds the layout for the footer.
- Ensure the output is fit for purpose and suitable for the audience.

Do **not** add any additional functionality.

Save your amended code file as **70 Read, analyse and refine programs Finished.py**   (7 marks)

# Convert algorithms 1

**1** This flowchart is for an algorithm that asks the user to input some information and then displays it back.

> Read the flowchart carefully. It contains information about how to name the variables and how to initialise them. It also gives you clues as to the data types of the expected inputs.

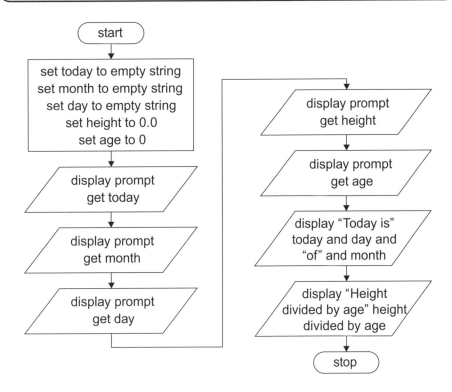

Open file **71 Convert algorithms 1 Student.py**

Write the code to implement the algorithm in the flowchart.

Do **not** add any additional functionality.

Save your amended code file as **71 Convert algorithms 1 Finished.py**

**(10 marks)**

# Convert algorithms 2

**1** This flowchart is for an algorithm that controls the opacity of a polymer dispersed liquid crystal window. When an electrical charge is applied, the crystals align to let light through. When there is no electrical charge, the crystals are scattered and the glass appears white so you cannot see through.

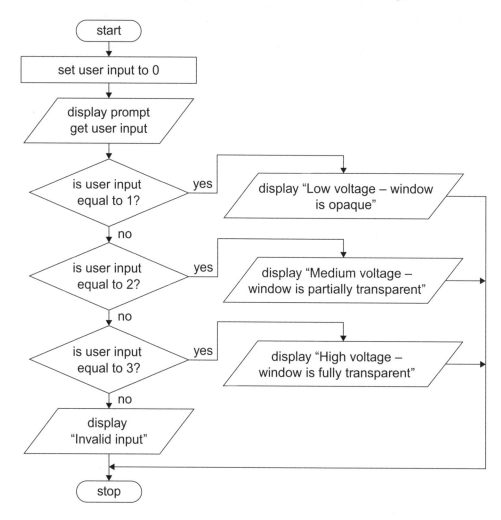

Open file **72 Convert algorithms 2 Student.py**

Write the code to implement the algorithm in the flowchart.

Do **not** add any additional functionality.

Add comments to explain your logic.

Use meaningful variable identifiers.

Save your amended code file as **72 Convert algorithms 2 Finished.py**          **(10 marks)**

When explicit directions are included in the question itself, make sure you follow them. For this question, make sure you include a few comments to explain the logic and use meaningful variable identifiers.

# Convert algorithms 3

**1** This flowchart is for an algorithm that generates a random number between 1 and 100 (inclusive). It then determines if the number is even or odd and reports that to the user. Users enter 'Q' when they want to exit the program.

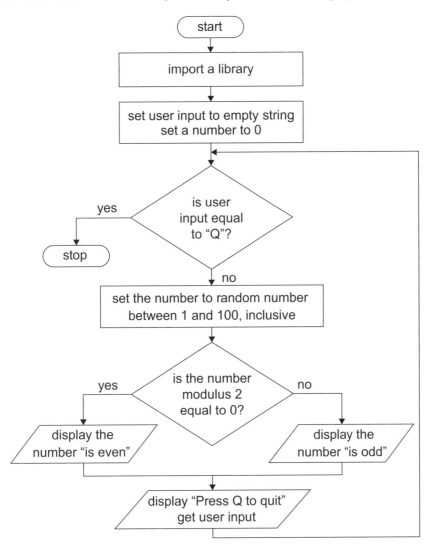

Open file **73 Convert algorithms 3 Student.py**

Write the code to implement the algorithm in the flowchart.

Do **not** add any additional functionality.

Add comments to explain your logic.

Use meaningful variable identifiers.

Save your amended code file as **73 Convert algorithms 3 Finished.py**          **(13 marks)**

> Notice in this flowchart that the user input must be 'Q', and not 'q'. You may think you need to add code to handle 'q', but the instructions state 'do not add any additional functionality'. You only need to translate the logic shown in the flowchart.

# Convert algorithms 4

**Target grade 4-6**

1 This flowchart is for an algorithm that displays the times tables for all numbers between 1 and 12, inclusive.

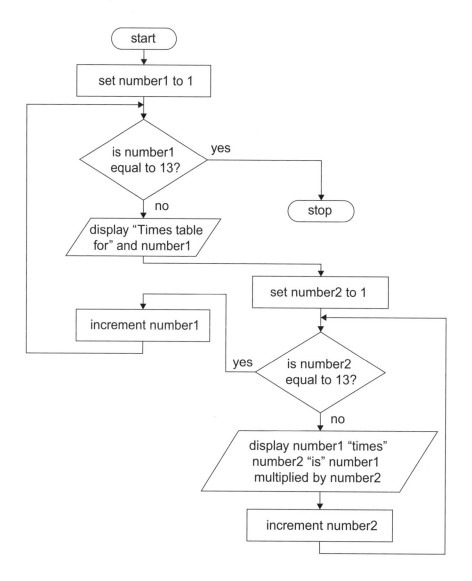

Open file **74 Convert algorithms 4 Student.py**

Write the code to implement the algorithm in the flowchart.

Do **not** add any additional functionality.

Save your amended code file as **74 Convert algorithms 4 Finished.py**    **(7 marks)**

The flowchart looks complex, but the solution is very simple. For this problem, work from the inside out. The right-hand side of the flowchart is an inner loop. The left-hand side of the flowchart is an outside loop. Both use the range() function.

# Convert algorithms 5

**1** This flowchart is for an algorithm that identifies the type of seafood that a user likes. The user is asked if they like each of the different varieties of seafood. The results are displayed for the user.

The varieties are stored as a one-dimensional data structure, implemented as a list.

```
varieties = ["lobster", "cuttlefish", "crab", "whelks",
             "scallops", "sea bass", "red mullet"]
```

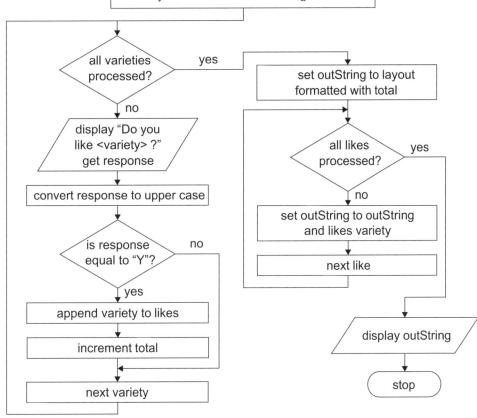

Open file **75 Convert algorithms 5 Student.py**

.PY

Write the code to implement the algorithm in the flowchart.

You must use the data structure provided.

Do **not** add any additional functionality.

Save your amended code file as **75 Convert algorithms 5 Finished.py**

**(15 marks)**

> This question starts you off with an existing data structure. In questions like this, you must use the data structure provided as it is. Do not be tempted to change it.

# Readability

Target grade **4-6**

**1** A program has been written to calculate the area and circumference of circles. The user chooses an option from a menu and provides the radius. The requested calculation is carried out and the result is displayed for the user.

Here is a sample console session.

```
------------------------------------------
 1 Area
 2 Circumference
 3 Exit
 Enter an option: 1
 Enter the radius of the circle: 10.4
 The area is 399.79466141227203
------------------------------------------
 1 Area
 2 Circumference
 3 Exit
 Enter an option: 2
 Enter the radius of the circle: 12.3
 The circumference is 77.28317927830892
------------------------------------------
 1 Area
 2 Circumference
 3 Exit
 Enter an option: 3
 Goodbye
```

Open file **76 Readability Student.py**

Amend the code to meet these requirements:

- Use layout to aid readability.
- Replace two variable names with more meaningful identifiers to explain the logic.
- Add at least **four** uses of white space to aid readability.
- Add at least **four** comments to explain the logic.
- Test the code with data appropriate to the context of the problem.

Do **not** add any additional functionality.

Save your amended code file as **76 Readability Finished.py**                    **(10 marks)**

> This question only requires you to change existing code, add white space, add comments and replace some variable names. Be careful not to change the functionality of the existing lines of code.

# Program errors

1 A programmer has started to write a program to count the number of females and males in a one-dimensional data structure. It does not work correctly. When the program is functioning correctly, it should output the numbers 3 and 7.

The console session output of the corrected program is shown here.

```
C:\Code\PycharmEnv\Scripts\python.exe
3
7

Process finished with exit code 0
```

Open file **77 Program errors Student.py**

Amend the code to:

- Fix the syntax error on the original line 1
  ```
  a = ["M", "M", "M", "M", "F", "F", "M", "F, "M", "M"]
  ```

- Fix the syntax error on the original line 7
  ```
  while (index <= length)
  ```

- Fix the syntax error on the original line 10
  ```
  ese:
  ```

- Change the identifier 'a' to a more meaningful name.

- Change the identifiers 'count' and 'count2' to more meaningful names.

- Fix the runtime error caused by the original line 7
  ```
  while (index <= length)
  ```

- Fix the logic error which causes the incorrect output.

- Add a comment to explain the original line 6
  ```
  length = len (a)
  ```

- Add at least one use of white space to aid readability.

- Ensure that the program produces the required output.

Do **not** add any additional functionality.

Save your amended code file as **77 Program errors Finished.py**    (10 marks)

> There is often a question like this towards the start of Paper 2. Remember, it is often a lot easier to change and correct code someone else has written than to write code yourself.

# Fitness for purpose and efficiency

**Target grade 7-9**

1   A program is being developed to provide information on how hot different types of chilli pepper are to eat. The heat of chilli peppers is measured in units on the Scoville scale.

Currently, the program reports:

- Any chilli pepper that has a space character in its name.
- The hottest chilli pepper and its Scoville measurement.

A console output is shown here.

```
Has space: Carolina Reaper
Has space: African Bird's Eye
Has space: Banana Pepper
The hottest pepper is Carolina Reaper at 1400000
```

In the future, the data contained in the program will be expanded. A search facility will be implemented. This will allow a user to type in a pepper name and find its Scoville measurement (if it is in the data).

Open file **78 Fitness for purpose and efficiency Student.py**

**.PY**

Amend the code to:

- Create a more efficient data structure.
- Design the data structure to make searching by name efficient in the future.
- Remove multiple 'if' statements.
- Ensure that the program produces the required output.

Do **not** add the search by name functionality.

Do **not** add any additional functionality.

Save your amended code file as **78 Fitness for purpose and efficiency Finished.py**

(10 marks)

> This question asks you to create a more efficient data structure. In the code file you will see that multiple variables are used to hold the pepper names and a one-dimensional data structure is used to hold all the heat measurements. A two-dimensional array would be a much more efficient way to hold all this data.

# Structural components of programs

1  A program uses turtle graphics to draw a grid for a game.

Open file **79 Structural components of programs Q1 Student.py**

Amend the lines at the bottom of the code to give:

- The name of a constant.
- The name of a global variable, with a string data type.
- The name of a data structure, implemented as a list.
- The name of a user-devised function.
- The name of a user-devised procedure.
- The name of a parameter.
- The name of a local variable.
- The line number(s) for a repetition.
- The line number(s) for an iteration.
- The line number(s) for a selection.

Do **not** add any additional functionality.

Save your amended code file as **79 Structural components of programs Q1 Finished.py**                                                          (10 marks)

> In questions that ask you to give line numbers, be careful with statements like 'if…elif…else', 'for…in range()', and 'while' because they include the indented lines as well. You can always give a range, such as 3 to 7, which includes the whole of the statement.

2  A program simulates the roll of a single die that can have a variable number of sides between six and ten (inclusive). The user inputs the number of sides.

Open file **79 Structural components of programs Q2 Student.py**

Amend the lines at the bottom of the code to give:

- The name of a library.
- The name of a constant.
- The name of a user-devised function.
- The name of a user-devised procedure.
- The name of a parameter.
- The name of a local variable.
- The line number(s) for a selection.
- The line number of a statement that changes the data type of a variable from integer to string.

Do **not** add any additional functionality.

Save your amended code file as **79 Structural components of programs Q2 Finished.py**                                                          (8 marks)

**Had a go** ☐    **Nearly there** ☐    **Nailed it!** ☐

# Iteration

**Target grade 4-6**

1   A program is needed to show how many students at a college are enrolled in foreign language classes. The data is stored in two data structures, implemented as lists. One holds the name of the language and the other holds the number of students enrolled in the class for that language. The number of students on the total roll is constant.

The output of the program is the name of each language, followed by the number enrolled, followed by the percentage of all students in the college enrolled in the class for that language. All percentages must be rounded to two digits after the decimal.

Some students do not take any language classes and some may take more than one language class, so the total of the percentages will not be 100.

> Notice that the names of the languages are stored in a list and that every language in the list must be processed. These facts indicate that you need to use iteration in your answer. You can do iteration with either a 'for … in' or a 'for … in range()' loop. Whichever you choose, make sure you process every item in the list in order.

This is what the output from the program should look like.

```
French 366 9.83
Italian 130 3.49
Spanish 494 13.27
Mandarin 79 2.12
German 243 6.53
Total for languages is 1312 35.25
```

Open file **80 Iteration Student.py**

Amend the code to produce the required output.

Do **not** add any additional functionality.

Use comments, white space and layout to make the program easier to read and understand.

Save your amended code file as **80 Iteration Finished.py**      **(10 marks)**

# Repetition

**1** A program is required to find the minimum, maximum and mean of a set of numbers entered by the user. The numbers can be between 0 and 500 (inclusive). Any number of numbers can be entered by the user. The end of the set is indicated when the user enters −1.

The user has to specify how many rounds they want to have, e.g. 2 rounds. In each round, the number of points is not set, so can vary. The user ends each round by entering a −1 for the points.

One round could have 4 scores and the second round could have 3 scores (as shown). The stats are reported for each round.

An example console session is shown.

```
How many different rounds? (0 to exit)) 2
Enter points scored (-1 to exit) 1
Enter points scored (-1 to exit) 2
Enter points scored (-1 to exit) 3
Enter points scored (-1 to exit) 4
Enter points scored (-1 to exit) -1
Max number: 4
Min number: 1
Mean number: 2.5
Enter points scored (-1 to exit) 153
Enter points scored (-1 to exit) 986
Enter points scored (-1 to exit) 521
Enter points scored (-1 to exit) -1
Max number: 986
Min number: 153
Mean number: 533.3333333333334
```

The program is being developed. Some sections of the program include different code options. Only one of the options in each section should be included in the program. Choose the options you want to keep by removing the # symbol(s). You can leave the other options as they are. You do not have to delete them.

Open file **81 Repetition Student.py**

**.PY**

Amend the code to make the program work and produce the correct output.

You will need to choose between alternative lines of code.

Do **not** change the functionality of the given lines of code.

Do **not** add any additional functionality.

Save your amended code file as **81 Repetition Finished.py**

**(7 marks)**

> When you are given a sample console session, you can use the information in it to test your code. In this case, type in the same input numbers and see if your program produces the same result. When it does, you will know your program is functioning correctly.

# Structured data types

1   A program is being developed to keep track of information about oysters. The
information includes the name of the oyster, the start of the harvesting season
and the end of the harvesting season. Boolean values indicate if the oyster is
available in small, medium or large sizes.

The required data is provided in comments at the top of the code file.

```
# Name, start of season, end of season, small, medium, large
#"Kyle of Tongue Pacific", "January", "December", 0, 1, 0
#"Loch Ryan Native", "September", "April", 0, 1, 1
#"Jersey Pacific", "January", "December", 0, 1, 0
#"Fal Native Oysters", "September", "March", 1, 1, 1
#"Porthilly Pacific", "January", "December", 1, 1, 1
#"Helford Native", "September", "April", 1, 1, 1
#"Cornish Native", "September", "March", 1, 1, 1
#"Teignmouth Wild Pacific", "January", "December", 0, 1, 1
#"Poole Pacific", "January", "December", 1, 1, 1
#"Whistable Pacific", "January", "December", 1, 1, 1
#"Maldon Wild Pacific", "January", "December", 0, 1, 1
#"Orford Pacific", "January", "December", 0, 1, 1
```

> In this question you are given data as comments in the top of the file.
> You are asked to create the data structure required. Take time to understand
> the types of data (integer, string, etc.) involved. This will help you
> determine the number of dimensions you need to use in your list.

Open file **82 Structured data types Student.py**

**.PY**

Amend the code to:

* Create a two-dimensional data structure to store the data.
* Complete the code for the shortSeason() subprogram.
* Use iteration ('for … in' loop) in the shortSeason() subprogram.
* Complete the code for the mediumOnly() subprogram.
* Use iteration (for … in range() loop) in the mediumOnly() subprogram.
* Ensure your program functions correctly.

Do **not** add any additional functionality.

Save your amended code file as **82 Structured data types Finished.py**    **(10 marks)**

> Iteration means processing every item in a data structure. You can do this
> with a 'for … in' or a 'for … in range()' loop.

# Data types, variables and constants

1 A program is being created to convert file sizes from kilobytes to kibibytes.

> Recall from Topic 2 that kibi is a base-2 prefix and represents 1024. Kilo is an International System of Units (SI) prefix and represents 1000.

The formula to convert from kilobytes to kibibytes is:

$$\text{kibibytes} = \text{kilobytes} \times 1000 \div 1024$$

Open file **83 Data types, variables and constants Student.py**

Amend the code to:

- Import the math library.
- Create a constant named KIBI and set it to 1024.
- Declare and initialise, separately, an integer variable to hold the size of a file.
- Create a real variable to hold the result of the calculation.
- Complete an input line to accept a value from the user.
- Calculate the file size using the correct formula.
- Complete the call to the math.ceil() function.

Do **not** add any additional functionality.

Save your amended code file as **83 Data types, variables and constants Finished.py**     **(10 marks)**

> Although this type of question has a lot of bullets to complete, once you open the student file, you will see that the outline of the program has been provided for you. There are clear directions for completing each bullet point. Look for the #=====> symbols that show you where to amend or write your code.

# String manipulation

**1**  A program is needed to validate a key that is entered by the user.

A valid key meets these requirements:
- Exactly five characters long.
- First two characters are alphabetic.
- First character is upper case.
- Second character is lower case.
- Last three characters are digits.

Test data for the program includes valid and invalid keys.

> In questions that provide test data, it is important to make sure that your program responds appropriately to all the data. At the very end, check all the data again to make sure you have not introduced errors.

| Valid keys are: | Invalid keys are: |
|---|---|
| • Ab123<br>• Qc865 | • Ab1234<br>• Ab&23<br>• 23789<br>• QB759<br>• Rw5R5 |

Open file **84 String manipulation Student.py**

Amend the code to check:
- The length of the input string.
- The input string for characters that are not alphabetic or digits.
- The input string for alphabetic characters only.
- The input string for upper case.
- The input string for lower case.
- The input string for digits.

Do **not** add any additional functionality.

Save your amended code file as **84 String manipulation Finished.py**    **(10 marks)**

# Input and output

**1** A program is needed to keep track of information about a class of students. A student record consists of a last name, a first name and four test scores. This information is stored as a two-dimensional data structure, implemented as a list.

The output from the program is a formatted table of results. There is no user input required.

Here is an example output, using the data in the data structure.

```
Last        First   T1 T2 T3 T4  Mean   Grade  Outcome
-----------------------------------------------------------
Lang        Carla   49 71 95 50  66.25  66     Pass
Bucklund    Pia     86 78 83 64  77.75  77     Pass
Lang        Jason   95 57 92 62  76.50  76     Pass
Dimitrousis Hector  93 45 89 96  80.75  80     Pass
Owens       Sunna   45 50 46 54  48.75  48     Fail
Goldin      Sandra  25 60 45 55  46.25  46     Fail
Giles       Seth    67 73 93 64  74.25  74     Pass
Gurillo     Melanie 88 88 62 79  79.25 * 79    Pass
Rykiel      Kari    67 92 54 86  74.75  74     Pass
Shailes     Dennis  56 70 84 62  68.00  68     Pass
```

The outcome for each student is reported as a pass or fail. A pass is awarded when the mean of the student's marks is 50 or greater. A fail is awarded when the mean of the student's marks is 49 or less.

As a pass can only be awarded if a student achieves 50 or more, a mean of 49.99 cannot be awarded a pass. Rounding is not allowed.

The program must:

- Use string constants for pass and fail.
- Calculate the mean of the test scores.
- Report the mean to two decimal places.
- Use the floor function to generate an integer grade not greater than the mean.
- Determine and report an outcome for each student.
- Work for any number of students in the class.

> In this question, you need to format the output so that it is fit for purpose and matches the table. It is more important that the program functions correctly than that every column is exactly formatted in line. Balance your time between all the requirements of the question.

Open file **85 Input and output Student.py**

Write a program to meet the requirements.

Do **not** add any additional functionality.

Use comments, white space and layout to make the program easier to read and understand.

Save your amended code file as **85 Input and output Finished.py**

**(15 marks)**

Had a go ☐    Nearly there ☐    Nailed it! ☐

# Read files

**Target grade 7-9**

**1** A program is needed to keep track of information about a shop's stock of sweets. The sweet record consists of a sweet name, the number of boxes in stock and the price per box.

This information is stored in a text file. The columns are: the sweet name, the number of boxes in stock and the price per box.

Here are the contents of the 'Sweets.txt' file. There are exactly 10 lines in the file. There are no blank lines.

```
Choco Drops,13,8.12
Aniseed Pyramids,18,2.11
Ice Cream Swirls,12,6.21
Caramel Bobs,16,4.94
Fluffy Clouds,14,5.61
Tangy Teeth,13,1.96
Minty,14,1.77
Cobblers,14,6.62
Chomps,12,4.63
Fruit Fizz,14,7.04
```

The program must:
- Read each line of the file.
- Convert the line to a record, implemented as a list.
- Calculate the current value of each sweet in stock by multiplying the number of boxes by the price per box.
- Round the current value to two decimal places, because this value is currency.
- Add the current value as an additional column into the record.
- Add the record to a two-dimensional data structure, implemented as a list.

Open file **86 Read files Student.py**

Write a program to meet the requirements.

Do **not** add any additional functionality.

Save your amended code file as **86 Read files Finished.py**

**.PY**

**(10 marks)**

> Notice that this question has no screen output. You might wonder how you will know it works. You have two choices. You can use your debugger to stop the code and look at the internal data structures or you can add in print statements to display the records as they are being built. Otherwise, you could print the first and the last record in the data structure to see if it matches the input data file. Although the instructions say 'do not add any additional functionality', the use of print statements does not change the overall functionality of the code and they are a good debugging tool. You can always comment them out after you have used them.

# Write files

**1** A program currently holds information about sweets in a shop. The data includes the sweet name, the number of boxes of each sweet in the shop and the purchase price of each box.

The information is held in a two-dimensional data structure, implemented as a list, inside the program.

Here are the contents of the sweetTable data structure.

```
sweetTable = [["Choco Drops", 13, 8.12],
              ["Aniseed Pyramids", 18, 2.11],
              ["Ice Cream Swirls", 12, 6.21],
              ["Caramel Bobs", 16, 4.94],
              ["Fluffy Clouds", 14, 5.61],
              ["Tangy Teeth", 13, 1.96],
              ["Minty", 14, 1.77],
              ["Cobblers", 14, 6.62],
              ["Chomps", 12, 4.63],
              ["Fruit Fizz", 14, 7.04]]
```

The program saves the data into a file named 'Sweets.txt'. Each record in the table is transformed into a line in the file. A field, showing the value of each sweet in stock, is added to the line.

Here are the contents of the 'Sweets.txt' file.

```
Choco Drops,13,8.12,105.56
Aniseed Pyramids,18,2.11,37.98
Ice Cream Swirls,12,6.21,74.52
Caramel Bobs,16,4.94,79.04
Fluffy Clouds,14,5.61,78.54
Tangy Teeth,13,1.96,25.48
Minty,14,1.77,24.78
Cobblers,14,6.62,92.68
Chomps,12,4.63,55.56
Fruit Fizz,14,7.04,98.56
```

The lines of code in the program are mixed up.

**Open file 87 Write files Student.py**

Amend the code to make the program work, so that it produces the correct output. You will need to rearrange the lines.

Do **not** change the functionality of the given lines of code.

Do **not** add any additional functionality.

Save your amended code file as **87 Write files Finished.py**

**(10 marks)**

> In questions where you are asked to use files as input, it is a good idea to make a backup copy of it before you start working with it. Sometimes, open files can be corrupted. If you have a backup copy, then you can reload it.

# Validation

Target
grade 1-3

1   A program is needed to validate user input. The program is partially complete, but the tests are not finished. The program needs length checks, presence checks, range checks and an equality check.

The rules for validating each input are shown in the table.

| Input | Rule |
|---|---|
| Name of a sandwich | Three to 20 characters in length |
| Number of the month | 1 to 12, inclusive |
| Any key | Cannot be blank |
| 3-dimensional axes labels | X, Y or Z |
| Asking for another round | Only 'y' or 'Y' should loop again |

Open file **88 Validation Student.py**

.PY

Amend the program to:

- Complete a **length** check of the sandwich name.
- Complete a **range** check of the month.
- Use a **presence** check to keep the user trapped in a loop.
- Use a **range** check of the axis label.
- Use an **equality** check to determine if the user wants to go again.

Do **not** add any additional functionality.

Save your amended code file as **88 Validation Finished.py**      **(10 marks)**

> In the student code file, you will notice that some of the lines of code you need to complete use nested brackets. Each set of inner brackets need a relational operator, such as <, <=, ==, etc. The space between the inner brackets needs a Boolean operator, such as 'and', 'or', or 'not'.

# Pattern check

1  A program is needed to validate a passkey entered by the user.

Valid passkeys:

- are exactly nine characters long
- contain only the digits 0 to 9 and the letters of the alphabet (either upper or lower case)
- contain exactly one special character from %, &, $, @, at any location.

This is the logic of the solution to the validation process:

- Ensure the passkey is nine characters long.
- Find the location of the special character.
- Copy all the characters, before the special character to a variable.
- Copy all the characters, after the special character to the same variable.
- Check that the contents of the variable are all alphanumeric.

> Alphanumeric characters only include the upper- and lower-case alphabet and the digits 0 to 9. A special character would cause the alphanumeric check to fail, so the program removes it.
>
> NB: the approach taken here is only one way of duplicating a string while leaving out part of it.

The program is partially written but is not complete.

**Open file 89 Pattern check Student.py**

.PY

Amend the program to complete:

- The subprogram that identifies the location of the special character.
- A call to the subprogram.
- The code to copy parts of the passkey.
- The code to check for digits and alphabetic characters.

Do **not** add any additional functionality.

Ensure the program works for all anticipated input.

**Save your amended code file as 89 Pattern check Finished.py**                    **(10 marks)**

> In questions like this, you cannot change the logic of the code, so you need to understand it fully. If the logic is not set out explicitly in the question, take a minute or two to read the entire student code file.

# Authentication

Target
grade **7-9**

**1** A program is needed to authenticate entry to a computer network. The user types in a username and a password. If these are found in the stored data, the user is asked an additional security question.

The data is stored in a two-dimensional data structure, implemented as a list. The columns are:

- Username – stored as a string.
- Passcode – stored as an integer, four digits long.
- Favourite biscuit – stored as a string.

**Open file 90 Authentication Student.py**

.PY

Write a program to meet these requirements:

**Inputs:**

- The username – no validation required.
- The passcode – must be four digits long.
- The biscuit name – no validation required.

**Processes:**

- Searches the table for matching name and passcode.
- Ensures the search works for any number of records in the table.
- Stops searching early if found.
- Stops searching early if the position where the name should be is passed over.
- Asks an additional security question if username and password found.

**Outputs:**

- Informative error messages to help the user correct their mistakes.

> From the description of the **processes**, you know that the data must be sorted and that you will need a Boolean flag to keep the 'passed over' state. You will also need to use a 'while' loop and a Boolean flag to keep the 'found' state. That way, the program will stop searching when 'found' is true or 'passed over' is true.

Do **not** add any additional functionality.

Use comments, white space, indentation and layout to make the program easier to read and understand.

Ensure the program works for all anticipated input.

Save your amended code file as **90 Authentication Finished.py**      **(15 marks)**

# Arithmetic operators

1 A program stores information about the lengths of the two sides of five different right-angled triangles. The information is stored in a two-dimensional data structure, implemented as a list.

Here is the data stored in the program.

```
triangleTable = [[22, 33],
                 [11, 66],
                 [66, 99],
                 [44, 88],
                 [99, 55]]
```

The output from the program is shown here.

```
A    B    C        Area
----------------------------
22   33    39.66    363.00
11   66    66.91    363.00
66   99   118.98   3267.00
44   88    98.39   1936.00
99   55   113.25   2722.50
```

> When you are asked to format outputs into columns or tables, you need to use the <string>.format() function. It allows you to align columns.
> In this output, the titles are left aligned, but the decimal numbers are all right aligned. Count off the characters in the columns to make sure you size them correctly.

The formulas needed for this program are:

$$\text{Area} = \frac{1}{2}\,ab$$

$$c = \sqrt{a^2 + b^2}$$

Open file **91 Arithmetic operators Student.py**

.PY

Write a program to produce the tabular output by processing the provided data structure.

Do **not** add any additional functionality.

Save your amended code file as **91 Arithmetic operators Finished.py**          (10 marks)

> In this question, you do not need to import the math library, because all of the arithmetic you need to do can be done using the operators you know. For example, you can find the square root of a number by raising it to the power of one half (1/2).

# Relational operators

Target
grade 1-3

**1** A program is required to determine if a temperature entered by the user (in degrees Celsius) is too hot, too cold or just right.

> When you are provided with input and output in a question, you can use them to test if your program is working correctly. Each output message will usually match a test condition using a relational operator.

Here is example input and output from a fully functional program.

| Temperature degrees Celsius | Output |
|---|---|
| −12 | Too cold |
| 0 | Too cold |
| 4 | Too cold |
| 5 | Just right |
| 6 | Just right |
| 29 | Just right |
| 30 | Just right |
| 31 | Too hot |

> This question does not state in the text what the boundaries are between too cold, just right and too hot. If you look carefully at the input and output given, you can see that the boundaries are between 4 and 5 and between 30 and 31.

Open file **92 Relational operators Student.py**

Amend the program to:

- Keep looping as long as the user responds with 'Y' or 'y'.
- Accept a temperature value from the user.
- Convert the temperature to an integer value.
- Report "Too hot" when the temperature is above 30°C.
- Report "Too cold" when the temperature is below 5°C.
- Report "Just right" in all other conditions.

Do **not** add any additional functionality.

Ensure the program works correctly for all anticipated input.

Save your amended code file as **92 Relational operators Finished.py**          **(7 marks)**

# Logical operators

1  A program is needed at a garden centre to select the correct fertiliser for plants.
The choice of fertiliser is based on the state and colour of the plants' leaves.
The user answers questions about the sick plant, selecting a number to represent
the symptoms they observe. The program then checks combinations of symptoms
and suggests fertilisers. The program may suggest more than one fertiliser or no
fertiliser at all. The user may choose to go around the program again.

> A question that includes a long description of the problem may not be
> complicated at all. This question just requires you to set up a series of test
> conditions to generate the required output. The logic to solve the problem
> is provided for you.

Here are the rules for the application of fertilisers.

| Fertiliser | Leaf colour | Leaf size | Leaf state | Tip colour |
|---|---|---|---|---|
| Nitrogen | Yellow | | | |
| Phosphorous | Brown | Small | | |
| Potassium | Brown | Normal | | |
| Calcium | | | Cracked/misshapen | |
| Magnesium | | | | Yellow |

Here is a console session from the complete program.

```
Would you like advice for a plant (Y/N)? y
What colour are the leaves (1) Green (2) Brown (3) Yellow: 2
What size are the leaves (1) Small (2) Normal: 2
What is the state of the leaves (1) Cracked/misshapen (2) Normal: 1
What colour are the tips of the leaves (1) Green (2) Yellow: 1
 Calcium Potassium
Would you like advice for a plant (Y/N)? n
Goodbye
```

Open file **93 Logical operators Student.py**

Amend the program to:

*   Keep looping as long as the user responds with a 'y' or 'Y'
*   Validate the selection of leaf colour
*   Validate the selection of leaf size
*   Validate the selection of leaf state
*   Validate the selection of tip colour
*   Complete the test condition for nitrogen
*   Complete the test condition for magnesium
*   Complete the test condition for calcium
*   Complete the test condition for potassium
*   Complete the test condition for phosphorous.

You must use the constants provided at the top of the file.

Do **not** add any additional functionality.

Save your amended code file as **93 Logical operators Finished.py**            (10 marks)

# Subprograms

**Target grade 7-9**

**1** A program is being developed by a student. The program is decomposed into three different parts, each with a different purpose.

Reverse printing of the alphabet.

- Use the range() function to generate integer values for the uppercase alphabet. The value for 'A' is 65 and the value for 'Z' is 90.
- Print the uppercase letter for each code in reverse order.
- Wait one second between letters.

> If you look in the built-in subprograms section of the Programming Language Subset (which you will be given in the exam) you will find the 'ord()' function which converts letters to their integer values. The 'chr()' function converts integers to letters.

Conversion of letter to ASCII code.

- Accept a letter inputted by the user.
- Validate the letter to be lowercase alphabetic only.
- Display a sentence giving the letter and its ASCII code.
- Use string concatenation to display the sentence.

Find the square root of a number.

- Accept a real number from the user.
- No validation is required.
- Display a sentence giving the number and its square root, rounded to four decimal places.

> Remember, taking a square root of a number is the same as raising the number to the power of one half.

Here is a console session from the fully functional program.
NB: more letters will be displayed than there is room to show here.

```
Z
Y
…
B
A
Enter a lowercase letter: w
Letter w is ASCII code 119
Enter a number: 135.2
The square root of 135.2 is 11.6276
```

Open file **94 Subprograms Student.py**

Write a program to meet the requirements.

Do **not** add any additional functionality.

Save your amended code file as **94 Subprograms Finished.py**     **(15 marks)**

**.PY**

# Functions

**1** A program is needed to display information about a sentence.

The program must meet these requirements:

- Accept a sentence from the user.
- Determine the length of the sentence.
- Use a subprogram to count the number of spaces in the sentence.
- Use a subprogram to count the number of vowels in the sentence.
- Each subprogram must take an input parameter and return a value.
- Each call to a subprogram must provide an input argument.
- Display the number of characters, the number of spaces and the number of vowels in the main program.

> Where the instructions are explicit and indicate you need subprograms, you should ensure you use them. If you cannot remember how to define subprograms (functions and procedures), look in the Programming Language Subset (PLS) document that you will have in the exam.

Here is a console session from the complete program.

```
Enter a sentence: The quick brown fox jumps over the lazy dog.
44 characters, 8 spaces, 11 vowels
```

Open file **95 Functions Student.py**

Write a program to meet the requirements.

Do **not** add any additional functionality.

Save your amended code file as **95 Functions Finished.py**

**(15 marks)**

> This is a high-mark question, the highest of any question in Paper 2. On such high-mark questions, make sure you use consistent design approaches. For example, use correct loop types and selection statements. Also ensure you use good programming practices, such as comments, white space and meaningful variables. Remember to make sure your program functions, even if it does not function perfectly.

Had a go ☐    Nearly there ☐    Nailed it! ☐

# Procedures

 **7-9**

**1** A program is needed to display information about a collection of children's books.

The data for all the books is stored in a two-dimensional data structure, implemented as a list. Information on each book is stored as a record. The fields in each record are: the book name, the price of the book and the number in stock.

Here is the data structure.

```
bookTable = [["Goldilocks", 3.67, 22],
             ["Little Bo Peep", 2.98, 14],
             ["Baa Baa Black Sheep", 3.32, 34],
             ["Jack and Jill", 4.51, 16],
             ["Twinkle Twinkle Little Star", 3.47, 25],
             ["Row Row Row Your Boat", 3.02, 18],
             ["Humpty Dumpty", 2.74, 14],
             ["Five Little Speckled Frogs", 2.83, 23]]
```

The program is required to display the information. It should use two separate subprograms.

- One subprogram to display the headers. This takes no parameters.
- One subprogram to display each book. This takes the data structure as a single parameter.

All columnar outputs should be formatted using <string>.format().

> In this question, you have been instructed to use <string>.format() to make sure all your columns line up properly. In the output image, you can see that the column headers are wider than the column data. This means you may have to try different inputs to the <string>.format() function to get the width and alignment right.

Here is a console session from the fully functional program.

```
Book                          Price      Volume
Goldilocks                    3.67       22
Little Bo Peep                2.98       14
Baa Baa Black Sheep           3.32       34
Jack and Jill                 4.51       16
Twinkle Twinkle Little Star   3.47       25
Row Row Row Your Boat         3.02       18
Humpty Dumpty                 2.74       14
Five Little Speckled Frogs    2.83       23
```

Open file **96 Procedures Student.py**

**.PY**

Write a program to meet the requirements.

Do **not** add any additional functionality.

Save your amended code file as **96 Procedures Finished.py**    (10 marks)

# Local and global variables

**1** A soft drinks company's visitor centre requires a program to suggest a random flavour for each visitor to taste.

An example output is shown.

> You should try the Grapefruit flavour soda.

The program has these requirements:

- The available flavours must be grapefruit, strawberry, lemon-lime, cherry and vanilla.
- The data on the flavours must be stored in a one-dimensional data structure, implemented as a list.
- The suggested flavour must be chosen at random.
- Concatenation must be used for displaying the output string.
- Only local variables must be used.

Open file **97 Local and global variables.py**

Amend the code to meet the requirements.

Do **not** add any additional functionality.

Save your amended code file as **97 Local and global variables Finished.py**    **(7 marks)**

> You need to read the requirements carefully. The last bullet is asking you to demonstrate your understanding of local variables.

# Timed test 1
# Principles of Computer Science

**Answer ALL questions.**
**In the exam, you will be given answer lines to write your response on.**
**Here you will need to write on your own paper.**

**Suggested time: 1 hour 30 minutes**

## 1 Data

(a) File sizes are measured in binary units of measurement.
Identify the largest unit of measurement. **(1)**

☐ **A** kibibyte

☐ **B** gibibyte

☐ **C** mebibyte

☐ **D** nibble

(b) Identify which of these denary numbers is represented by the binary number 0111 0101. **(1)**

☐ **A** 105

☐ **B** 110

☐ **C** 117

☐ **D** 156

(c) Identify which of these binary numbers is represented by the hexadecimal number A7. **(1)**

☐ **A** 1010 0110

☐ **B** 1010 0111

☐ **C** 1011 0111

☐ **D** 1100 1110

(d) A bitmap image is represented as a grid of pixels.

   (i) State what is meant by the term 'pixel'. **(1)**

   (ii) The image is 780 pixels high and 580 pixels wide and has a 24-bit colour depth.
   Construct an expression to calculate the file size of the image in kibibytes. **(4)**

   (iii) Lossy compression is often used to reduce the file size of images.
   Describe how lossy compression reduces the size of a file. **(2)**

(e) Describe how ASCII represents text. **(3)**

(f) An analogue-to-digital converter (ADC) changes the analogue signal from a microphone
to a digital signal for the computer to process.

   (i) Describe the process of converting a sound from analogue to digital. **(3)**

   (ii) A digital sound recording is 90 seconds long. It has a sample rate of 44.1 kHz and
   a bit depth of 32-bits.

   Construct an expression to calculate the file size of the sound in mebibytes.
   You do not have to do the calculation. **(4)**

**(Total for Question 1 = 20 marks)**

## 2 Networks

Being connected on a network enables computers to communicate with each other.

(a) LANs and WANs are two types of network.

Describe how a LAN differs from a WAN. **(2)**

(b) Give **two** distinct types of transmission media used to connect devices on a network. **(2)**

(c) Protocols play an important role in network communication.

   (i) State the purpose of a protocol. **(1)**

   (ii) Identify the protocol used to transfer data in networks. **(1)**

      ☐ **A** CPU

      ☐ **B** DNS

      ☐ **C** ISP

      ☐ **D** TCP/IP

(d) Data is split up into packets for transmission across the internet.

A header is attached to each packet.

Two items in a packet header are a sequence number and a checksum.

   (i) Explain the purpose of the sequence number. **(2)**

   (ii) Describe how the checksum is used to identify packets that have been corrupted in transit. **(3)**

(e) The star network topology has a high degree of fault tolerance.

Explain **one** reason a star topology is fault tolerant. **(2)**

(f) Describe how a firewall protects a company network from external cyberattacks. **(2)**

**(Total for Question 2 = 15 marks)**

## 3 Issues and impact

(a) A bank uses a machine-learning algorithm to determine the credit worthiness of people applying for a loan.

   (i) Describe how a machine-learning algorithm is taught. **(3)**

   (ii) The bank discovers that the algorithm unfairly discriminates against certain individuals.

     Give **two** possible reasons for this algorithmic bias. **(2)**

(b) Jacob has invented a new type of smartphone battery and has applied for a patent.

   (i) Describe how a patent will protect Jacob's intellectual property (IP). **(2)**

   (ii) Jacob hopes his invention will reduce the amount of energy consumed by smartphones.

     Explain **one** way energy consumption by digital devices harms the environment. **(2)**

**(Total for Question 3 = 9 marks)**

## 4 Computers

(a) Give **one** reason the 'stored program' concept is regarded as a major breakthrough in the development of computers. **(1)**

(b) Two components used in the fetch-decode-execute cycle are the address bus and the data bus.

   (i) Describe **one** reason the data bus is bidirectional. **(2)**

   (ii) Describe **one** reason the address bus only needs to be unidirectional. **(2)**

(c) An embedded system in a smart light bulb automatically adjusts the brightness of the bulb according to the ambient light in the room.

Describe how the embedded system achieves this. **(3)**

(d) A word processing application on Joe's computer needs to print a document.

Describe the role of the operating system in printing the document. **(2)**

(e) A team of programmers is about to start work on a new project.

Discuss what the team should do to ensure that their software is robust.

Your answer should consider: good programming practice, code reviews and audit trails. **(6)**

**(Total for Question 4 = 16 marks)**

## 5 Computational thinking

(a) Here is the list of countries Stephen has visited on holiday.

| Peru | Laos | Gambia | India | Algeria | Fiji |
|------|------|--------|-------|---------|------|

The list is to be sorted into ascending order using a bubble sort. Five passes are needed.

Complete the table to show the stages of the bubble sort. **(4)**

| Peru | Laos | Gambia | India | Algeria | Fiji |
|------|------|--------|-------|---------|------|
|      |      |        |       |         |      |
|      |      |        |       |         |      |
|      |      |        |       |         |      |
|      |      |        |       |         |      |
|      |      |        |       |         |      |

(b) Complete the truth table for the operation

P AND (Q OR NOT R) **(3)**

| P | Q | R | NOT R | Q OR NOT R | P AND (Q OR NOT R) |
|---|---|---|-------|------------|---------------------|
| 0 | 0 | 0 |       |            |                     |
| 0 | 0 | 1 |       |            |                     |
| 0 | 1 | 0 |       |            |                     |
| 0 | 1 | 1 |       |            |                     |
| 1 | 0 | 0 |       |            |                     |
| 1 | 0 | 1 |       |            |                     |
| 1 | 1 | 0 |       |            |                     |
| 1 | 1 | 1 |       |            |                     |

(c) Here is an algorithm that searches a list.

```
1       searchList = ["Alex", "Calum", "David", "Maddy", "Pete",
2                     "Rosie", "Tim"]
3
4       name = "Josie"
5
6       first = 0
7       last = len(searchList) - 1
8       mid = 0
9       found = False
10
11      while ((first <= last) and (not found)):
12          mid = (first + last) // 2
13          if (searchList[mid] == name):
14              found = True
15          else:
16              if name < searchList[mid]:
17                  last = mid - 1
18              else:
19                  first = mid + 1
20
21      if (not found):
22          print (name, "is not in the list.")
```

State the value of the variables first and last when line 13 is executed and searchList[mid] holds the value of "David".

first .................................................................

last .................................................................

(d) A transport company pays its drivers an annual bonus.

Full-time drivers are paid £100 for each year of service, up to a maximum of £500.
Part-time drivers are paid £50 for every full 100 hours worked, up to a maximum of £300.

Complete the flowchart to show the process of determining the bonus for a driver. **(6)**

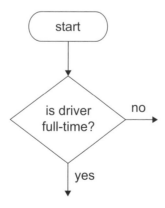

**(Total for Question 5 = 15 marks)**

**TOTAL FOR PAPER = 75 MARKS**

**101**

Had a go ☐    Nearly there ☐    Nailed it! ☐

# Timed test 1 – Answers

**1 Data**

(a) B – gibibyte

(b) C – 117

(c) B – 1010 0111

(d) (i) The smallest item of information in a bitmap image.

    (ii) $(780 \times 580 \times 24) \div (8 \times 1024)$.
        $780 \times 580 \times 24$; $\div$; 8; 1024.

    (iii) Some of the data is permanently removed, which means that the file cannot be fully restored to the original.

(e) A 7-bit binary code is used, allowing 128 unique binary patterns to be generated, enough to represent all the lower- and upper-case English characters, the numbers 0–9 and punctuation marks.

(f) (i) The amplitude/height of the analogue signal is sampled at fixed points in time and encoded as a binary number.

    (ii) $(90 \times 44.1 \times 1000 \times 32) \div (8 \times 1024 \times 1024)$.
        $90 \times 44.1 \times 32$; $\times 1000$; $\div$; $8 \times 1024 \times 1024$.

**2 Networks**

(a) A LAN connects computers over a small geographical area, often on a single site, whereas a WAN connects LANs together and spans multiple sites over a larger geographical area.

(b) Two of: air/wireless/radio waves, copper wire, fibre-optic cable.

(c) (i) The purpose of a protocol is to enable networked devices to communicate with each other by establishing a set of rules that all must follow.

    (ii) D – TCP/IP.

(d) (i) The sequence number is used to reassemble packets in the correct order, because packets travel to their destination via different routes and may be out of sequence on arrival.

    (ii) A checksum formula is applied to the packet before it leaves the source and the resulting checksum is added to the packet header. The same checksum formula is reapplied when the packet reaches its destination and compared with the checksum in the packet header. If they do not match, a resend request is issued.

(e) If one node or cable connection fails, the rest of the network is unaffected and continues to function, because every node is connected via a dedicated cable to the central node/switch.

(f) A firewall monitors incoming traffic and blocks any originating from an unrecognised or blacklisted source.

**3 Issues and impact**

(a) (i) The algorithm initially learns from training data that specifies what the correct outputs are for certain individuals and groups. The more data that is fed in, the more the performance of the algorithm improves.

    (ii) Unrepresentative/insufficient data may have been used to train the system. The algorithm may reflect the prejudices/bias of the software engineers who developed it.

(b) (i) It will give Jacob the right to stop others from making, using or selling his invention without his permission for 20 years.

    (ii) Most of the energy used is produced from burning carbon-based fossil fuels, which scientists believe is contributing to global warming.

## 4 Computers

(a) Being able to store instructions in memory meant that computers could perform a variety of tasks without having to be rebuilt or rewired each time.

(b) (i) Instructions and data are transferred along the data bus from memory into the CPU for processing. The results of operations carried out in the CPU are transferred along the data bus in the opposite direction to be stored in memory.

(ii) The address bus only needs to pass on memory addresses from the CPU to memory, because its sole purpose is to identify the address of the location in memory that is to be read from or written to.

(c) A sensor inputs ambient light levels, which are compared with stored light levels. An actuator then adjusts the brightness up or down accordingly.

(d) The application hands the print task over to the operating system, which sends the instruction to the printer using the printer's own driver.

(e) Your answer could include some of the following ideas:

- The team should agree a code of practice and a set of standards that must be adhered to. This will make it easier for them to read each other's code and to integrate subprograms written by different team members.

- They should agree that only third-party library subprograms with no known security vulnerabilities are to be used. They should build in sufficient time for testing.

- The team should set up and maintain an audit trail. They should use version control software to keep track of who made what changes to the code and when. This will mean that, should an issue come to light, the code can be rolled back to a point before the problem was introduced.

- An external expert should be appointed to carry out regular code reviews, inspecting the code for instances of bad programming practice and code vulnerabilities.

## 5 Computational thinking

(a)

| Peru | Laos | Gambia | India | Algeria | Fiji |
|---|---|---|---|---|---|
| Laos | Gambia | India | Algeria | Fiji | Peru |
| Gambia | India | Algeria | Fiji | Laos | Peru |
| Gambia | Algeria | Fiji | India | Laos | Peru |
| Algeria | Fiji | Gambia | India | Laos | Peru |
| Algeria | Fiji | Gambia | India | Laos | Peru |

(b)

| P | Q | R | NOT R | Q OR NOT R | P AND (Q OR NOT R) |
|---|---|---|---|---|---|
| 0 | 0 | 0 | 1 | 1 | 0 |
| 0 | 0 | 1 | 0 | 0 | 0 |
| 0 | 1 | 0 | 1 | 1 | 0 |
| 0 | 1 | 1 | 0 | 1 | 0 |
| 1 | 0 | 0 | 1 | 1 | 1 |
| 1 | 0 | 1 | 0 | 0 | 0 |
| 1 | 1 | 0 | 1 | 1 | 1 |
| 1 | 1 | 1 | 0 | 1 | 1 |

(c) first = 2
last = 2

(d)

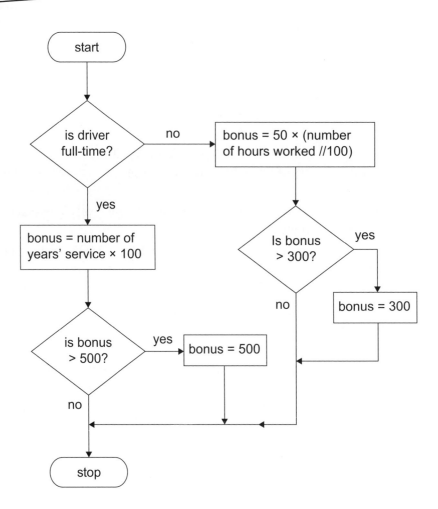

# Timed test 2
# Application of computational thinking

**Answer ALL questions.**

**Suggested time: 10 minutes**

1   A program determines if a customer is entitled to a discount on a meal. If the customer is a child, with an age between 1 and 13 (inclusive), the meal is half price. If the customer is over 60 years old, the senior discount is 20%.

Open file **Timed test 2 q1.py**

Amend the code to add or complete lines to:

- Create one constant.
- Create one variable.
- Accept the user's input and assign it to a variable.
- Determine if the customer is entitled to a half-price meal.
- Determine if the customer is entitled to 20% off a meal.
- Display a message appropriate for a senior discount.

Do **not** add any additional functionality.

Save your amended code file as **Q01_FINISHED.py**

**(Total for Question 1 = 10 marks)**

**Suggested time: 20 minutes**

2   A programmer has started to write a program for a rock, paper, scissors game, but it does not work correctly.

Open file **Timed test 2 q2.py**

Amend the code to:

- Fix the syntax error on original line 10

  ```
  SCISSORS == "SCISSORS"
  ```

- Fix the syntax error on original line 20

  ```
  computerChoice = choices[random.randint (0, 2)
  ```

- Fix the logic error on original 26

  ```
  if computerChoice != PAPER:
  ```

- Fix the logic error on original line 36

  ```
  if computerChoice == SCISSORS:
  ```

- Change the identifier 'u' to a more meaningful name

- Add a comment to explain why the user input is converted to upper case on original line 22

  ```
  u = u.upper ()
  ```

- Add at least one use of white space to aid readability.

Do **not** add any additional functionality.

Save your amended code file as **Q02_FINISHED.py**

(Total for Question 2 = 7 marks)

**Suggested time: 20 minutes**

3  The flowchart below is for an algorithm that calculates the length of the hypotenuse (c) of a right-angled triangle.

The user enters the length of two sides (a, b) of the triangle.

The numbers are positive real numbers larger than 0.

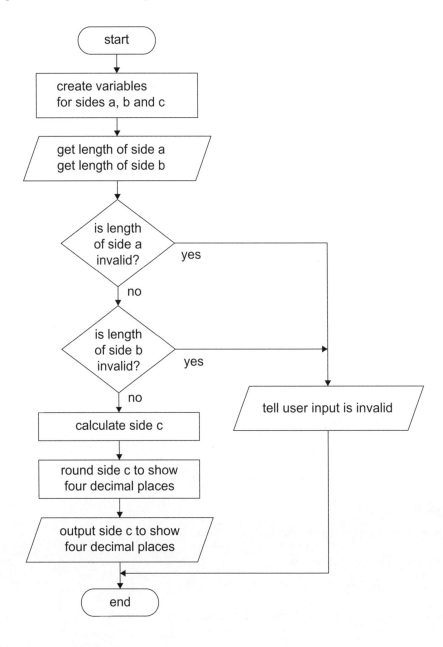

The length of the hypotenuse is calculated using the formula:

$$c = \sqrt{a^2 + b^2}$$

The square root can be calculated raising a number to the power of ½.

There is no need for the math library.

Open file **Timed test 2 q3.py**

Write the code to implement the algorithm in the flowchart.

Do **not** add any additional functionality.

Use comments, white space and layout to make the program easier to read and understand.

Save your amended code as **Q03_FINISHED.py**

(Total for Question 3 = 15 marks)

**Suggested time: 20 minutes**

4  A program is being developed to draw a smiley emoji. The output should look like this image.

The program will output the smiley emoji in colour, as follows:

- The face is filled with yellow.
- The eyes are filled with white.
- The arc for the smile is red.
- All other lines and shapes are black.

The lines of code in the program are mixed up.

Open file **Timed test 2 q4.py**

Amend the code to make the program work and produce the correct output. You will need to rearrange the lines.

Do **not** change the functionality of the given lines of code.

Do **not** add any additional functionality.

Save your amended code file as **Q04_FINISHED.py**

(Total for Question 4 = 13 marks)

**Suggested time: 25 minutes**

5   A program is being developed to work with a one-dimensional data structure of random numbers. The data structure is implemented as a list.

The random numbers are generated by a subprogram and placed into the list.

A subprogram is required to calculate the mean of the even numbers in the data structure.

Open file **Timed test 2 q5.py**

Amend the program and subprogram to meet the following requirements:

- The subprogram must be named 'evenMean'.
- The subprogram must take one and only one parameter.
- The subprogram must calculate the mean of the even numbers only.
- The subprogram must return the mean to the caller.
- The subprogram must work for any number of values generated.

Do not add any additional functionality.

Save your amended code as **Q05_FINISHED.py**

(Total for Question 5 = 15 marks)

**Suggested time: 25 minutes**

6   Menu options for meat eaters and vegetarians are stored in a two-dimensional data structure, implemented as a list. Each record in the data structure has a field for the name of an option and the price of that option. The last field is 'true', if the option is vegetarian and 'false' if it is not.

A program is needed to separate the options into two different comma-separated value text files, one for meat eaters and the other for vegetarians.

The file format is the same for both files.

Each record in the file consists of the name and price, separated by a comma.

The vegetarian file already has records in it which must be retained.

Open file **Timed test 2 q6.py**

Write a program to meet the following requirements:
- Append all the vegetarian options to the vegetarian file.
- Write all the meat options to the meat file.

Do **not** add any additional functionality.

Use comments, white space and layout to make the program easier to read and understand.

Save your amended code as **Q06_FINISHED.py**

(Total for Question 6 = 15 marks)

**TOTAL FOR PAPER = 75 MARKS**

# Timed test 2 – Answers

**1** Your answer code should include/do the following:

- Create a constant.

  ```
  SENIOR = 60
  ```

- Create a variable.

  ```
  age = 0
  ```

- Accept user's input.

  ```
  Use of input ()0
  Conversion of string to integer
    [age = int (input ("Enter your age in full years: "))]
  ```

- Complete conditional tests for child.

  ```
  Check for bottom boundary
  Check for upper boundary
  Boolean operator to combine
    [if ((age >= 1) and (age <= 13)):]
  ```

- Complete conditional test for senior.

  ```
  Relational operator
  Use of constant
    [elif (age > SENIOR):]
  ```

- Display a senior message.

  ```
  print ("20% off your meal.")
  ```

Completed solution is in **Q01_MARK_SCHEME.py**

**2** Your answer code should include/do the following:

- Fix the syntax error (line 10) by changing == to =.
- Fix the syntax error (line 20) by adding the missing ].
- Fix the logic error (line 26) by changing != to ==.
- Fix the logic error (line 36) by changing SCISSORS to ROCK.
- Change identifier 'u' to a more meaningful name, such as 'userChoice', throughout.
- Add a comment to explain why user input is converted to upper case, e.g. "Convert to upper case to match the choices defined in the list of constants, which are all in uppercase".
- Add at least one blank line/white space to aid readability, e.g. between inputs and processing.

Completed solution is in **Q02_MARK_SCHEME.py**

**3** Your answer code should include/do the following:

- Creation of three variables, one for each side.
- All side length variables are data type real.
- Layout, indentation, comments, white space and meaningful identifiers used to aid readability.
- Two inputs are taken from the user.
- String inputs from the user converted to real.
- Selection is used to identify invalid input.

- Appropriate message for invalid input.
- Range check on both variables being less than or equal to 0.
- Boolean operator used to combine range checks into a single statement/nesting of range checks.
- Calculation translated correctly.
- Side c rounded to four decimal places.
- Side c printed to four decimal places using <string>.format.
- Accurate use of relational operators (=>, <=) in appropriate selection or sequence statements.
- Accurate use of arithmetic operators (*, **) in calculation.
- Program should produce the correct output for any predictable input.

Completed solution is in **Q03_MARK_SCHEME.py**

**4** Your answer code should include/do the following:

- import turtle is topmost line of file.

drawEye subprogram:

- defined in subprogram area.
- sends all direction to 'inTurtle', i.e. no 'tim'.
- inTurtle.penup () is last line.
- draws an eye.

face decomposition:

- tim.penup () before set position.
- tim.pendown () before tim.circle ().
- mouth is red.
- face is yellow.

drawing eyes:

- white part of eyes must be drawn before black part.
- eyes are white and black.
- creation of tim placed after subprogram.
- hiding turtle is last line.

Completed solution is in **Q04_MARK_SCHEME.py**

**5** Your answer code should include/do the following:

Subprogram to calculate even mean:

- Defined using def.
- One single parameter.
- Local variable for total.
- For loop iteration to process all items.
- Relational operator used to identify even number.
- Modulus used to identify even number.
- Mean calculated using division.
- Mean calculated using count of even numbers.
- Mean returned.
- Translates without syntax or runtime errors, even if reduced functionality.
- Functions properly for 100 generated values.
- Functions properly for any number of items in initial list.

- Only local variables used in solution.
- Mean variable initialised to real value, if declared.
- Total initialised to integer 0. Count of numbers initialised to 0.

Completed solution is in **Q05_MARK_SCHEME.py**

6   Your answer code should include/do the following:

- Open meat file for 'writing'.
- Open vegetarian file for 'appending'.
- Close both files before existing program.
- Indexing used to access fields in each record.
- Comma added between fields.
- Line feed added to end of output line.
- Use of 'for' loop to iterate over a data structure, rather than a 'while' loop.
- Conversion of data types to those required by program, e.g. reals become strings.
- Write in a high-level language.
- White space is used to show different parts of the solution/functionality.
- Variable names are meaningful.
- Comments are provided and are helpful.
- Use of selection to decide which file to use.
- Files' contents are accurate for all records.
- Functions correctly for any number of options in the list.

Completed solution is in **Q06_MARK_SCHEME.py**

| These are the contents of the completed vegetarian file. | These are the contents of the completed meat file. |
|---|---|
| Mujadara,4.88<br>Shakshuka,5.98<br>Shatta,1.35<br>Adas bil Hamod,5.55<br>Baba Ghanouj,5.37<br>Batata Harra,5.66<br>Fattoush,4.44<br>Hummus,5.12<br>Manakish,5.05<br>Tabbouleh,5.11 | Kafta,7.74<br>Kanafeh,7.61<br>Kibbeh,8.03<br>Sfeeha,8.91<br>Sheikh Mahshi,8.91<br>Shish Taouk,8.28 |

# Answers

## 1. Decomposition and abstraction

1 Your answer could include three of the following:
- Record user move.
- Check for winner.
- Check for draw.
- Get user's move.
- Make computer move.
- Get symbol for first move.
- Any other task that might be in the game.

2

| Item | Must be kept | Can be abstracted away |
|---|---|---|
| The colour of the cover | | ✓ |
| The International Standard Book Number (ISBN) | ✓ | |
| The shelf location | ✓ | |
| The subject area | ✓ | |
| The type of cover (hard or paper) | | ✓ |

## 2. Using subprograms

1 A self-contained block of code that performs a specific task.

2 Your answer could include some of the following ideas.

Decomposition:
- Each subprogram is the solution to a small part of a larger problem.
- Each subprogram is designed to accomplish only a single well-defined task in a larger solution.
- Subprograms can be reused by calling, rather than recreation, just like a building block in a larger solution.

Abstraction:
- The code/programmer using the subprogram does not have to know how it works on the inside.
- The subprogram should be named in such a way that its name indicates its role in the solution.

- Subprograms can call subprograms, so the programmer can achieve higher and higher levels of abstraction to simplify problem solving, hiding ever more implementation details.
- Subprograms use arguments/parameters so that the programmer can move parts of solutions to different problems/contexts.

## 3. Algorithms: flowcharts

1 ( start ) ( stop )

Accept alternative labels: start/stop, begin/end.

2 This symbol shows a subprogram that has its own flowchart.

3 Your flowchart should include:
- Start and stop symbols with appropriate labels.
- A Process symbol to initialise at least one variable.
- An Input symbol with instruction to get/receive user input.
- An Output symbol with instruction to print/display result of number doubled (any method).
- Arrows connecting all the symbols in sequence.

## 4. Algorithms: selection

1 B

2 One mark for each, for a maximum of 4.
- Both A and B tests use the variable named 'choice'.
- Both A and B tests use relational operators, but they must be different
  - >= "A" and <= "Z"
  - <= "Z" and >= "A"
- Both A and B tests are clearly phrased to indicate a question, for example, by starting with the word 'is' and ending with a '?' or both.
- Order of tests must be correct for yes/no labels.

Examples:

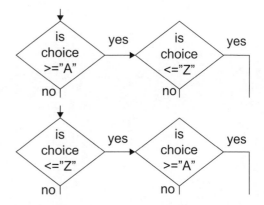

# 5. Algorithms: repetition

1 (a) Your description could include the following:

- Finds out how many items the customer has bought.
- Adds up the total cost of items bought in a loop.
- Checks to see if the customer gets a discount.
- Applies the discount if earned.
- Tells the customer how much to pay.

(b) is numItems == 0?

# 6. Algorithms: iteration

1 Your flowchart should include:

- Loop to process each row in the table.
- Loop to process each number in the row.
- Totals for each row and grand total calculated correctly.
- All selection/loop symbols have one entry point and two exit points.
- All exits from loop test have yes/no/true/false labels.
- Algorithm functions as required in the context of the problem.

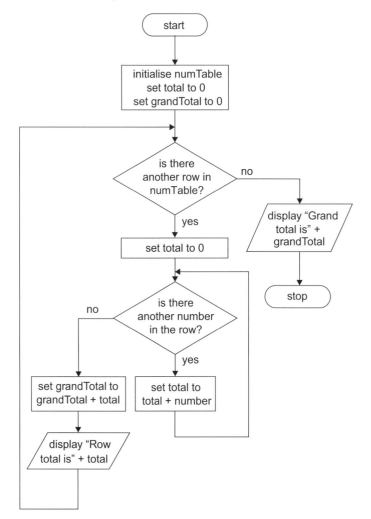

# 7. Variables and constants

1 (a) A variable is a container that is used to store values so that they can change as the program is running.

(b) The value stored in a variable can change during program execution, whereas the value of a constant always stays the same.

(c) They should be given meaningful names so that anyone reading the code will be given an indication of the types of value they are intended to contain, e.g. 'studentAge' rather than just 'X'.

(d)

| Variable | Use within the program |
|---|---|
| mysteryNumber | This is used to hold the number which must be guessed. |
| correct | This is a 'flag' used to indicate whether the guess matches mysteryNumber. |
| guess | This is used so that the user can enter a number. |

# 8. Arrays

1 (a) An array is a data structure that can store multiple items/elements of data that are all of the same data type.

(b) (i) 6

(ii) 36.7

(iii) Iteration/loop/for/while.

2

|   | 0 | 1 | 2 | 3 |
|---|---|---|---|---|
| **0** | 1 | 0 | 0 | 1 |
| **1** | 0 | 1 | 1 | 0 |
| **2** | 0 | 0 | 0 | 0 |
| **3** | 0 | 1 | 1 | 0 |

# 9. Records

1 (a) Similarity: both store multiple data items in one single structure.

Difference: in an array, all items must be of the same data type. In a record, each item can be a different data type.

(b) (i) Records allow fields of different data types, such as weight and name, whereas arrays would only allow fields of the same type.

(ii) The column headings are not part of the data structure.

## 10. Arithmetic and relational operators

1 (a) Relational operators are used to make comparisons.

  (a) Repetition/while/selection/if.

2

| Statement | True or False |
|---|---|
| 14 // 3 < 4 | False |
| 2**3 >= 8 | True |
| 12 + 6 / 2 == 15 | True |
| 6 * (8 / 2) > (6 * 8) / 2 | False |
| 23 % 6 != 5 | False |

## 11. Logical operators

1 The cells should read from top to bottom.

- Out of range [NB: already provided]
- Number is acceptable
- This would be OK
- These numbers are OK.

## 12. Determining correct output

1 (a) To create login names for the students of a school.

  (b) Their first name, family name, intake year and tutor group.

  (c) The variable 'check' acts as a pointer indicating which element of the array 'names' will be looked at next.

  (d) 18CooperRBlue is unique.

## 13. Using trace tables

  (a) Array

  (b) (See table below)

## 14. Errors that can occur in programs

1

| Error line number | Correction |
|---|---|
| 7 | terri.setposition (100, 100) |
| 11 | terri.forward (75) |
| 12 | terri.right (90) |
| 17 | terri.pensize (2 * DEFAULT_ PENSIZE) |
| 19 | for count in range (3): |

## 15. Linear search

1 (a) A linear search algorithm starts at the beginning of a list and moves through it, item by item, until it finds the matching item or reaches the end of the list.

  (b) A brute-force algorithm tries out every possibility until a solution is found or all possibilities are exhausted.

  (c) This algorithm uses a 'for' loop to look at every item in the list, therefore, all items after the found one would still be looked at.

## 16. Binary search

1 Each pass discards half the data. The same algorithm is then repeated on the remaining part.

2 The data must be sorted for a binary search/the data is not in alphabetical order.

3

| Sublist | Median calculation | Median item |
|---|---|---|
| Ahmad Ava Emma Josiah Mateo Maya Paru Stephen Zoey | (8 + 0) // 2 = 4 | Mateo |
| Maya Paru Stephen Zoey | (8 + 5) // 2 = 6 | Paru |
| Stephen Zoey | (8 + 7) // 2 = 7 | Stephen |

| target | found | index | numList[index] | output |
|---|---|---|---|---|
| 13 | False | | | |
| | | 0 | 5 | |
| | | 1 | 9 | |
| | True | 2 | 13 | |
| | | 3 | 2 | |
| | | | | The item is in the list |
| | | | | |

## 17. Bubble sort

**1**

|  | 20 | 15 | 3 | 13 | 9 | 2 | 6 |
|---|---|---|---|---|---|---|---|
| **Pass 1** | 15 | 3 | 13 | 9 | 2 | 6 | 20 |
| **Pass 2** | 3 | 13 | 9 | 2 | 6 | 15 | 20 |
| **Pass 3** | 3 | 9 | 2 | 6 | 13 | 15 | 20 |
| **Pass 4** | 3 | 2 | 6 | 9 | 13 | 15 | 20 |
| **Pass 5** | 2 | 3 | 6 | 9 | 13 | 15 | 20 |
| **Pass 6** | 2 | 3 | 6 | 9 | 13 | 15 | 20 |

**2**  Two/2

**3**  One/1

## 18. Merge sort

**1**  Each small 'sub-problem' is easier to solve than one large problem. It is more efficient to combine the solutions than to try to solve the main problem without using any techniques.

**2**

| 33 | 25 | 46 | 2 | 8 | 69 | 9 |

| 33 | 25 | 46 | 2 | | 8 | 69 | 9 |

| 33 | 25 | | 46 | 2 | | 8 | 69 | | 9 |

| 33 | | 25 | | 46 | | 2 | | 8 | | 69 | | 9 |

| 25 | 33 | | 2 | 46 | | 8 | 69 | | 9 |

| 2 | 25 | 33 | 46 | | 8 | 9 | 69 |

| 2 | 8 | 9 | 25 | 33 | 46 | 69 |

## 19. Efficiency of algorithms

**1**  Bubble sort is a simple algorithm to learn, whereas merge sort is a complex algorithm, which involves recursion.

You might also say: Bubble sort is good for short lists, which students can hardcode, whereas merge sort is better for long lists, which are difficult for students to work with.

**2**  (a)   1.......50.......100 first median is 50

1.......**25**........**49** second median is 25

1.......**12**........**24** third median is 12

1.......**6**.........**11** fourth median is 6

1.......**3**..........**5** fifth median is 3

1.......**1**..........**2** sixth median is 1

There is only one number left (number 2) to select and therefore the maximum number of selections is 7.

(b)  Data in a binary search must be sorted, which takes time. A linear search could find the item in a small list faster. A linear search would find the item quickly if it were the first item, whereas a binary search would still have to do all the splitting, which could take longer.

## 20. Logical operators

**1**

| Input | | Output |
|---|---|---|
| 0 | 0 | 0 |
| 0 | 1 | 1 |
| 1 | 0 | 1 |
| 1 | 1 | 1 |

**2**  (a)   (A OR B) AND NOT (C)

(b)

| A | B | C | P |
|---|---|---|---|
| 0 | 0 | 0 | 0 |
| 0 | 0 | 1 | 0 |
| 0 | 1 | 0 | 1 |
| 0 | 1 | 1 | 0 |
| 1 | 0 | 0 | 1 |
| 1 | 0 | 1 | 0 |
| 1 | 1 | 0 | 1 |
| 1 | 1 | 1 | 0 |

## 21. Using binary

**1**  A processor consists of billions of transistors, each of which has just two states, on/off.

The on/off states of a transistor represent the binary digits 0/1.

**2**  C ($2^4 = 16$).

**3**  010, 011, 100, 101, 110, 111.

**4**

| 1 | 0 | 1 | 1 |
|---|---|---|---|
| 8 | 0 | 2 | 1 |

**5**  A bit is short for binary digit, the smallest unit of data in a computer. A bit has a single binary value, either 0 or 1.

## 22. Unsigned integers

**1** 1100 0111

**2** Decimal = 128 + 16 + 4 + 2 + 1 = 151

**3** The denary number 256 would be represented in binary as 1 0000 0000 and so would need 9 bits to store it.

## 23. Two's complement signed integers

**1**

| | | | | | | | | |
|---|---|---|---|---|---|---|---|---|
| 0 | 0 | 1 | 1 | 0 | 1 | 1 | 0 | Start with +54 |
| 1 | 1 | 0 | 0 | 1 | 0 | 0 | 1 | Flip each of the bits from 1 to 0 and 0 to 1 |
| 0 | 0 | 0 | 0 | 0 | 0 | 0 | 1 | Add a binary 0000 0001 |
| 1 | 1 | 0 | 0 | 1 | 0 | 1 | 0 | Result is –54 in two's complement |

**2**

| | | | | | | | | |
|---|---|---|---|---|---|---|---|---|
| 0 | 1 | 0 | 1 | 0 | 1 | 1 | 1 | Original pattern 0101 0111 |
| 1 | 0 | 1 | 0 | 1 | 0 | 0 | 0 | Flip each of the bits from 1 to 0 and 0 to 1 |
| 0 | 0 | 0 | 0 | 0 | 0 | 0 | 1 | Add a binary 0000 0001 |
| 1 | 0 | 1 | 0 | 1 | 0 | 0 | 1 | This is the correct result. |

The student's answer of 1011 1001 is incorrect. The incorrect answer is generated by adding 0001 0001 instead of 0000 0001.

**3**

| | | | | | | | | |
|---|---|---|---|---|---|---|---|---|
| 1 | 1 | 1 | 0 | 1 | 1 | 1 | 1 | Original pattern |
| 0 | 0 | 0 | 1 | 0 | 0 | 0 | 0 | Flip bits |
| 0 | 0 | 0 | 0 | 0 | 0 | 0 | 1 | Add 1 |
| 0 | 0 | 0 | 1 | 0 | 0 | 0 | 1 | Result –17 |

## 24. Binary addition

**1**

```
  0   1   0   1   0   1   1   1
  0   1   0   1   1   1   1   1
 ¹1   0  ¹1  ¹1  ¹0  ¹1  ¹1   0
```

**2** Incorrect

```
  0   1   0   1   0   1   1   1
  0   1   0   0   1   0   1   0
 ¹1   0  ¹1  ¹0  ¹0  ¹0   0   1
```

**3** (a) 0000 0000 (one mark for each nibble)

(b) 28

(c) –28

## 25. Logical and arithmetic shifts

**1** An arithmetic shift preserves the sign/most significant/leftmost bit, whereas a logical shift always fills the vacated bits with 0s.

**2**

| Shift | Result |
|---|---|
| Logical right shift of four places | 0000 1110 |
| Logical left shift of two places | 1011 0000 |
| Arithmetic right shift of three places | 1111 1101 |
| Arithmetic left shift of one place | 1101 1000 |

**3** (a)

| Binary number | 1010 1101 | Decimal equivalent | 173 |
|---|---|---|---|
| Binary number after a two-place logical right shift | 0010 1011 | Decimal equivalent | 43 |

(b) In a two-place logical right shift, the binary number is divided by 4. The result of dividing 173 by 4 is 43.25. The right shift produces an imprecise result because it discards the two rightmost bits of the binary number. and effectively rounds down to the nearest whole number.

## 26. Overflow

**1** An error that occurs when a calculation produces a result that is greater than the computer can store, or is greater than the number of bits available to store it.

**2** The program might crash.
Further use of the incorrect result in calculations will cause further errors.

**3** 0101 0100. Note that the overflow is not part of the answer.

**4** (1) 0011 0001

**5** Shifting left the original pattern 1100 0011, gives 1000 0110. The original 1 in the most-significant bit is shifted out, therefore using a position that does not exist in the register.

## 27. Hexadecimal

**1** (a) Hexadecimal is used because people get confused with large binary numbers. Binary numbers can be simplified by writing them in hexadecimal as fewer numbers are needed.

(b) A8 is equal to the denary numbers 10 and 8. 10 and 8 represent the two nibbles of the binary number.
Therefore the binary number = 1010 and 1000 = 1010 1000.

(c) (i) 1101 0101 = the two nibbles 1101 and 0101.

These are equal to the two denary numbers 13 and 5.

Therefore the hexadecimal number = D5.

(ii) 1011 1101 = 1011 and 1101 = 11 and 13 = BD.

# 28. Characters

1 The character set is the list of binary codes that can be recognised by the computer hard- and software.

2 Your answer might mention the following points:

- ASCII is a 7-bit code.
- There are 128 code sequences representing English characters and control actions such as SPACE and SHIFT.
- The codes are grouped according to function, e.g. codes 65 to 90 represent the uppercase letters of the alphabet.

3 The first sentence is made up of all English characters so can be represented in 7-bit ASCII, whereas the second sentence has foreign characters which do not fit into 7-bit ASCII.

4 72

# 29. Bitmap images

1 (a) The size of an image is given as the number of pixels in its width (W) and height (H).

The resolution of an image is the number of pixels per unit area of the display.

(b)

| Colour depth | Number of colours represented |
|---|---|
| 1 | 2 |
| 3 | 8 |
| 8 | 256 |

(c) File size = W × H × colour depth
= 2000 × 3000 × 24
= (2000 × 3000 × 24) ÷ (8 × 1024 × 1024)

# 30. Analogue sound

1 (a) The sample rate describes the number of sound samples that are taken each second.

(b) Increasing the sample rate gives a more accurate reproduction of the analogue wave, as more samples are taken with less time between them.

2 (a) The bit depth describes the number of bits used to encode the data taken in each sample.

(b) A high bit depth allows more data to be stored and allows the dynamic range of the sound to be more accurately represented.

3 Length of recording and number of channels (e.g. mono or stereo).

4 File size (bits) = sample rate × bit depth × recording length = (44100 × 16 × 100) ÷ (8 × 1024 × 1024)

# 31. Limitations of binary data representation

1 000, 001, 010, 011, 100, 101, 110, 111.

2 $2^n$

3 C – 7

4 The increase in the number of colours available using 8 bits may not be needed in the application because the slight improvement in quality may not matter to the person viewing the image. The image may be on a web page that is transferred over the internet, which needs to load very quickly. The higher colour depth file would take longer to transfer and load more slowly.

5 Reducing the bit depth reduces the file size and so the audio file will transmit faster. Reducing the bit depth reduces the number of distinct values and these may not be noticed by the human ear.

# 32. Binary units of measurement

1 D – they are base 2

2

| Order | Unit |
|---|---|
| Smallest | bit |
| ↓ | nibble |
| | byte |
| | kibibyte |
| | mebibyte |
| | gibibyte |
| Largest | tebibyte |

3 Division by 8
Division by 1024
Division by 1024
Division by 1024
72 000 000 000 ÷ (8 × 1024 × 1024 × 1024)

4 (5312 × 2988 × 16) ÷ (8 × 1024 × 1024)

## 33. Data compression

1  (a)  Any two of the following.
- It uses less internet bandwidth when they are sent and received.
- The transfer speed is quicker.
- The files take up less storage space on their computers.

(b)  Lossless compression reduces file sizes without deleting any data. When the file is decompressed, it is exactly the same as the original. Nothing is lost. Lossless compression looks for redundancy, where the same data is stored many times, and groups this data into one reference in the file.

Lossy compression reduces the file size by deleting some data. The original can never be reconstituted when it is decompressed as it has been irreversibly changed.

(c)  (i) PDF file: lossless.

The novel would be impossible to read if some of the data (words) were removed permanently.

(ii) Images of her trip to London: lossy.

Areas with very similar colours are merged into one to reduce file size. People cannot distinguish these small differences and so are not aware that the data has been removed.

## 34. The stored program concept

1  Program instructions and data.
2  Memory/RAM. Input and output mechanisms.
3  Locations in memory can be accessed directly in any order.
4  C – Control unit.

## 35. The central processing unit

1

| Hardware component | Function |
|---|---|
| Control unit (CU) | Fetches program instruction from main memory, decodes them and directs the operation of all the other parts of the system to execute them. |
| Clock | Controls the rate at which program instructions are executed. |
| Arithmetic logic unit (ALU) | Performs arithmetic and logic operations. |
| Registers | Provides direct-access storage for instructions, intermediate results and data within the CPU. |

2  A: Clock. B: Address bus. C: Data bus. D: ALU. E: Registers
3  The higher the clock speed, the more instructions a CPU can execute per second, because every CPU requires a fixed number of clock ticks to execute an instruction.

## 36. The fetch-decode-execute cycle

1 (a)

| Description | Order |
|---|---|
| The next instruction is sent from the RAM to the CPU. | 2 |
| The instruction is carried out. | 4 |
| The CU decodes the instruction. | 3 |
| The CPU sends a signal to the RAM requesting the next instruction. | 1 |

(b)  RAM is where the program instruction and data are stored while they are needed.

(c)

| CU (control unit) The CU **decodes** the instructions. If a calculation is needed, the CU instructs the **ALU**. |  | ALU (arithmetic logic unit) **Calculations** are carried out in the ALU. |
|---|---|---|

2  Registers store data within the CPU so that it can be accessed very quickly. Some registers perform special functions, e.g. storing the memory address for the next instruction. Others are general purpose.

3  The memory address 0101 1101 is put onto the address bus. Next, the CU sends a read signal down the control bus. Finally, the instruction stored in memory location 0101 1101 is placed on the data bus and transferred to the CPU.

## 37. The need for secondary storage

1

| Description | Primary storage | Secondary storage |
|---|---|---|
| Non-volatile | | ✓ |
| Directly accessible by the CPU | ✓ | |
| Storage over 1 TiB | | ✓ |

2 The application, together with any files for use in that application, are loaded into memory from secondary storage. When a file is saved, it is transferred from memory to secondary storage. When the application is closed, it is removed from memory.

3 Secondary storage enables programs to be stored for as long as they are needed. This means that programs can be loaded into main memory and executed as required, without having to be keyed in each time.

## 38. Types of secondary storage

| 1 | Type | Description |
|---|------|-------------|
| | Magnetic | Uses metal platters coated in iron oxide. The platters rotate at high speed. |
| | Optical | Small pits are burned in patterns onto a flat surface. A laser can be used to interpret light reflected from the flat or pitted surface. |
| | Solid state | No moving parts; data is stored as an electrical charge. |

2 Any two from:
- Lighter/more portable
- No moving parts that could be damaged if the laptop is dropped
- Fast data access speeds
- Quieter
- More energy efficient.

3 (a) A laser is used to burn the surface of the disk so that it becomes more reflective or less reflective. The data is stored as a series of lands (reflective areas) and pits (less reflective areas) in a single track that spirals out from the centre of the disk.

(b) Any two from:
- Cheap
- Sufficient capacity to store the video
- Portable.

## 39. Embedded systems

1 A small computer on a chip, that performs a dedicated task within a bigger system.

2 Any three from:
- Microcontroller
- Sensors
- Battery
- Actuator
- Timer

- Counter
- Receiver/transmitter
- Analogue-to-digital converter.

3 Sensors woven into the fabric of the t-shirt measure key metrics. A Bluetooth transmitter is used to stream data from these sensors to the phone.

## 40. Operating system 1

1 A scheduling algorithm is used by the OS to ensure that all processes get a share of CPU time/can progress towards completion.

2 An active process is one that is loaded into memory and is being executed by the CPU. An inactive process is one that is waiting in the queue for its turn to use the CPU.

3 Virtual memory is an area of the hard drive. It is used by the OS to temporarily store inactive processes when RAM becomes full. When they are needed again, the processes are transferred back into RAM.

4 A paging algorithm is used by the OS to decide which memory pages to swap out to RAM/which memory addresses to assign to which process.

## 41. Operating system 2

1 A device driver provides an interface that allows the OS to communicate with a peripheral device.

2 (a) Lola should have read access to the design drawings, because she needs to be able to refer to them but does not need to alter them.

(b) Erik should have execute access to email software, because he needs to be able to use email to keep in touch with colleagues and clients.

(c) Lola should have delete/full access to the article, because she needs to be able to edit it and even delete it (if she decides not to submit it for inclusion in the newsletter).

## 42. Utility software

1 (a) A hard drive is said to be fragmented when it is no longer able to store a complete file in one location and has to split it up and put parts of it in gaps between existing files wherever space is available.

(b) Defragmentation software rearranges the files on the disk so that the file blocks that belong to a single file are moved closer together. This means that there are fewer disk accesses needed to read the data.

(c) (i) When he is attaching a file to an email or uploading it to a website.

(ii) Lossless compression reduces the file size without discarding any of the data and allows the original file to be restored when it is decompressed, whereas lossy compression reduces the file size by discarding some of the data, so the original file cannot be restored when it is decompressed.

2   One method identifies malware by comparing its definition/signature with definitions/signatures stored in a database of known malware. Another method uses a set of rules to detect suspicious behaviour, which would suggest that a file could be malware.

## 43. Robust software

1   Robust software:
   • can handle unexpected actions without crashing or producing incorrect output
   • is free from security vulnerabilities that could be exploited by hackers.

2   The code reviews will identify problems while the code is being developed. This means that problems with the code, and any non-adherence to agreed practices, can be addressed immediately before any further development takes place.

3   An audit trail keeps track of every change made to the software. This means that code can be rolled back to a state before the error was made.

## 44. Programming languages

1   Any three from:
   • Resembles human language
   • Machine-independent
   • Problem-oriented
   • Has a high level of abstraction
   • Must be translated into machine code in order to be executed
   • Comes with libraries of ready-made functions, integrated development tools, etc.

2   In assembly language, instructions are written as mnemonics and translated to machine code, whereas programs written in machine language (binary) need no translation.

3   Programs written in a high-level language are likely to be less efficient, use more operations and consume more memory than ones written in a low-level language. This is because the program will not be optimised to make the most of the features of a particular CPU.

## 45. Interpreters and compilers

1   (a) Assembler

   (b) A compiler translates the source code into a stand-alone machine code program/object code as a one-off process, whereas an interpreter translates the high-level code line by line each time the program is run.

2   On a set-top receiver, an executable code produced by a compiler will execute much more quickly than code, which has to be translated prior to being executed.

3   Evie should use an interpreted language to learn to program for a number of reasons.

   It will be simpler/quicker for her to test and debug her programs, because errors are reported as they occur. A compiler would collate a list of errors encountered during translation but would only report them once translation was complete.

   It will be easier for Evie to make amendments to her programs if she uses an interpreted language. A compiled language would require her to revisit the original source code and recompile it once she had finished making changes.

   Speed is unlikely to be an issue for Evie, so the fact that programs written in an interpreted language run more slowly than those that have been compiled is not a deciding factor. Similarly, portability and code optimisation are not likely to be major considerations in this instance.

## 46. Networks

1   Any two from::
   • To share files and data.
   • To share resources such printers and hard drives.
   • To share an internet connection and internet services, such as web-based software.
   • To deploy software and patches.
   • To provide centralised support and backup services.
   • To enable people to communicate using services such as email and video conferencing.
   • To enable people to work collaboratively while being geographically remote from each other.

2   (a) A LAN:
      • covers a relatively small geographic area, often a single site
      • is, typically, privately owned
      • is usually managed by a network manager or team at the site.

(b) A WAN:
- spans multiple sites over a large geographical area
- connects separate LANs to form a network of networks
- uses infrastructure that is owned and maintained by several different organisations.

3 Data from the sensors is sent via the LAN to the monitoring device. The monitoring device uses the WAN to contact the police and the LAN to switch on the siren.

## 47. The internet

1 An IP address is needed to uniquely identify the device on the internet.

2 (a) URL stands for uniform resource locator. It is the complete web address of a particular web page, image or other resource on the internet.

(b) The domain name of the website is part of the URL. Domain names are user-friendly versions of IP addresses, which are easier for humans to remember and type in.

3 The DNS server translates the domain name part of the URL into its equivalent IP address. This enables the browser to request the web page from the web server where it is hosted.

## 48. Packet switching

1 (a) A data packet is a small amount of data sent over a network. It consists of a header, a payload and a footer.

(b) Any three from:
- IP address of destination.
- IP address of source.
- Sequence number.
- Total number of packets.
- Checksum.

(c) You should give a linked description that makes reference to any four of the following:
- Data packets are transmitted across the internet using a technique called packet switching.
- Routers forward packets between networks.
- When a router receives a packet, it looks up the destination address in the packet header.
- A router uses its routing table to decide where to send it.
- Routers keep each other informed of any traffic holdups so that they can avoid sending packets along congested routes.
- A packet will need to be forwarded between several routers before it reaches its destination.

## 49. Wired versus wireless

1 (a) Bandwidth is the volume of data that can be transmitted across a transmission medium in a given time.

(b) Latency is the time lag between data leaving its source and arriving at its destination.

2 (a) Any two from:
- Visitors and employees can connect to the network easily.
- Visitors and employees can connect their own digital device(s) to the network, and can move around the building without losing the connection.
- A wireless network is easy and quick to install.

(b) A wired network is only accessible from within the building using a secure physical cable connection, whereas in wireless networks the Wi-Fi signal is broadcast inside and outside the building, leaving it vulnerable to hackers.

## 50. Connectivity on a LAN

1 (a) The transmission medium is the communication channel through which data is sent from one device to another across on a network.

(b) The wireless signal is susceptible to interference from other wireless networks or devices, such as microwaves.

(c) A NAS drive attached to a home network may be used to stream video and music files to connected devices. This requires higher transfer speeds and lower latency than is reliably provided by a wireless connection.

2 Your answer might include three of the following:
- Radio waves are used to send and receive data.
- Devices such as mobile phones and tap-to-pay credit/debit cards are used to make payments.
- A specialised NFC card reader is used.
- The sender must be in close proximity to the card reader in order to make a contactless payment.
- The card reader can only connect to one payment device at a time.
- Encrypted data is exchanged between the sender and reader to complete a payment.

## 51. Network speeds

1 bits per second (bps)

2 $(1.2 \times 1024 \times 1024 \times 1024 \times 8) \div (15 \times 60 \times 1000)$

3 $(286 \times 1024 \times 1024 \times 8) \div (3.2 \times 1000 \times 1000 \times 1000)$

4 $(5 \times 60) \times (6.8 \times 1000 \times 1000 \times 1000) \div (1024 \times 1024 \times 8)$

## 52. Network protocols

1 Protocols enable the devices connected to the network to communicate with each other, because they define the rules that govern how data must be formatted, transmitted and received on a network.

2 Data sent using HTTP between a user's browser and the server that hosts Anja's website is not encrypted, which means that potentially sensitive information could be stolen in transit. HTTPS addresses this by creating a secure encrypted connection between the server and the browser.

3 IMAP retains the email on a server enabling it to be read on any device, whereas POP3 deletes the data after it has been downloaded to the client so that is not then possible to access it from a different computer

## 53. The TCP/IP model

1 A protocol stack is a hierarchical set/stack of network protocols that enables devices to communicate with each other over the internet.

2 (a) Any two of: FTP, HTTP, HTTPS, SMTP, POP, IMAP.

   (b) Ethernet, Wi-Fi.

3 (a) TCP splits outgoing data into packets and numbers them. It also adds a header to each packet.

   (b) IP adds the source and destination IP addresses to the header of outgoing packets.

## 54. Network topologies

1 The topology of a network describes how devices are physically arranged and connected together.

2

| Characteristic | Bus | Star | Mesh |
|---|---|---|---|
| Each device is connected to a central switch | | ✓ | |
| Each device has a dedicated connection to one or more other devices | | | ✓ |
| Each device is connected to a central cable | ✓ | | |

3 Each node is connected to at least one or more other nodes. This means that if one node fails, or a connection is broken, traffic can be rerouted a different way.

4 All the devices on a bus network are connected to a single cable. Since only one device at a time can transmit data along the cable, the more devices that are added to the network, the more frequently data collisions will occur and the slower the network will become.

## 55. Network security

1 (a) An ethical hacker is a security expert employed by a company to try to find security vulnerabilities in its network.

   (b) Penetration testing is when networks are put under deliberate attack in order to identify any weaknesses and vulnerabilities, so that they can be fixed.

2 Your answer could include some of the following. (See the levels-based mark scheme for how questions like this are marked.)

   • All organisations rely on the data stored on their networks; without it they are not able to function.

   • The aim of network security is to protect an organisation's data by ensuring only authorised users can access the network and its resources.

   • Threats can originate from outside the organisation. Hackers will try to find loopholes in security to launch a cyberattack. Penetration testing is an important weapon in identifying gaps in security.

   • The actions of people who work for the organisation can also pose a security threat to security. The principle of least privilege is used to limit the amount of damage they can do. This involves giving employees only the level of access to files that they need to do their job.

   • Security breaches can be very expensive in terms of business disruption and financial losses. Extra costs may also be incurred if, for example, hackers extort money by encrypting files or threatening to reveal sensitive information.

   • Theft of business-critical data may have serious financial implications if, for example, new product details were leaked to a competitor.

   • A major data breach will damage an organisation's reputation. Customers will be very annoyed and many are likely to switch to another supplier. This may be hard for the company to recover from.

   • The secure storage of personal data (such as names, addresses and health and financial information) is a legal requirement under the Data Protection Act. Organisations risk substantial fines and compensation claims for any data breaches that occur.

## 56. Protecting networks

1 (a) Your answer might include some of the following points:

   • Keep the room locked.

   • Install closed-circuit TV to monitor people going in and out of the room.

   • Install an alarm system.

- Use automated lighting in the room so that lights go on when someone enters and turn off when they leave.
- Physically attach equipment to the building (e.g. bolt it to the floor).
- Put bars across any windows.

(b) (i) Your answer might include two of the following:

- Fingerprint recognition.
- Facial recognition.
- Voice recognition.
- Retina scan.
- Iris recognition.

(ii) With a keypad system, an authorised user could accidentally or deliberately give away their PIN, allowing a hacker to enter the server room. Biometric identification relies on the physical characteristics of an individual. These characteristics are very hard to fake or steal.

(c) Consultants should only be given permission to read employee records. They should not be given permission to edit or delete them. Human resources staff should be given full access rights, enabling them to enter, edit and delete employee records.

# 57. Environmental issues 1

1 Your answer could include one of the following:

- Large quantities of raw materials are used in the manufacturing process. Many, including copper and palladium, are non-renewable. Some, including arsenic and cadmium, are highly toxic.
- Mining scars the landscape with unsightly waste heaps and damages wildlife habitats.
- Most of the energy used in the manufacturing process comes from non-renewable fossil fuels. This contributes to global warming.
- Polluted waste water is a by-product of the manufacturing process. It can seep into groundwater and harm plants and animals.

2 Your answer could include two of the following:

- The disposal of digital devices in a landfill causes harm because dangerous chemicals could leak into and pollute groundwater.
- Burning e-waste to separate out reusable materials damages the environment because harmful chemicals can be released into the atmosphere.
- Reclaiming precious metals from e-waste can be harmful because it can expose workers to dangerous chemicals.

- The incineration of digital devices could cause air pollution because dangerous chemicals can be released into the atmosphere.

3 Your answer could include three of the following:

- Responsible recycling recovers valuable and non-renewable metals.
- It recovers many other types of reusable materials.
- It disposes of dangerous devices responsibly.
- It reduces the potential for chemical leakage and fires in landfills.
- It leads to less e-waste being transported overseas.

# 58. Environmental issues 2

1 Your answer could include one of the following:

- Intelligent traffic control systems reduce fuel consumption, because they keep traffic moving efficiently and prevent congestion.
- Smart lighting systems reduce energy consumption, because they switch off lights when there is no one in the room.
- Environmental surveillance protects endangered species, because it can spot suspicious activity in a national park and alert law enforcement agents.
- Data collection and analysis can reduce food waste, because it can help charities work with supermarkets to direct surplus food to people who need it.
- Engine management systems in modern cars use sensors to optimise fuel consumption and reduce of carbon dioxide emissions.

2 (a) Your answer could include one of the following:

- She can take her laptop to the retailer where she bought it. The retailer is obliged to take it back and recycle it.
- She can donate it to a charity that refurbishes IT equipment and sends it to a developing country.
- She can take it to a recycling centre that harvests reusable components.

(b) Your answer could include three of the following:

- Make it a legal obligation for manufacturers to design digital devices that are repairable and upgradable.
- Improve the energy efficiency of digital devices.

- Use efficiency settings to reduce power usage.
- Site data centres in areas where they can be powered and cooled by renewable energy.

## 59. Personal data

1 Personal data is information that relates to an identified or identifiable individual.

2 Personal data is a valuable source of information about customers' purchasing habits and preferences. It helps retailers to customise the offers they make to customers. This results in increased sales and better customer retention.

3 Your answer could include two of the following:
- Her location can be pinpointed at any time.
- Detailed data about her movements, the places she visits, etc., is stored on her phone. This data could be passed on to a third party without her knowledge.
- It could make her a target for stalking and make her vulnerable to attack.
- It could mean that she will be inundated with targeted ads.

4 Data may be shared with other companies, because it is unclear who owns it.

## 60. Legislation

1 (a) Data Protection Act.
  (b) Your answer could include three of the following:
  - To be informed about the collection and use of their data.
  - To access their data.
  - To have inaccurate data corrected.
  - To have data erased (i.e. be forgotten).
  - To restrict the way in which their data is processed.
  - To obtain and reuse their personal data for their own purposes.
  - To object to how their data is processed.
  - To withdraw consent at any time.
  - To complain to the Information Commissioner.
  (c) Your answer could include three of the following:
  - To inform people how the data is being used.
  - Not to use the data for anything other than the specified purpose.
  - To keep the data secure.
  - Not to collect any more data than is necessary.
  - Not to keep the data any longer than necessary.

- To ensure that the data is accurate and up to date.
- Not to use the data for any other purpose without our consent.

2

| Action | Type of offence |
|---|---|
| A student accesses another student's email account without permission. | A |
| A black-hat hacker exploits a security loophole in the school's network to launch a ransomware attack. | C |
| A student accesses their parents' stored credit card numbers and security codes in order to buy goods online without their permission. | B |
| A student guesses the login names and passwords of other students and logs into their accounts to read their emails. | A |
| A computer science student successfully guesses the network manager's password. He uses it to gain access to the school's data management system and deletes all the staff records. | C |

## 61. Artificial intelligence (AI)

1 Artificial intelligence is the general term for computer systems that exhibit intelligent behaviour and are capable of performing tasks normally associated with humans.

2 Your answer could include one of the following:
- The system's algorithm could have become biased because the real-world data used to train the system was biased.
- Bias could be amplified because there could be a design flaw in the algorithm.
- The developers who built the system may have unintentionally incorporated their own prejudices and preconceptions into its design.

3 The algorithms in machine-learning systems are programmed to learn to make autonomous decisions. This makes it impossible to attribute the decisions a system makes to a particular individual or group.

4 Narrow AI is a system that is only capable of performing a single or limited task or a limited range of tasks. Such systems cannot transfer their knowledge to another domain. They fail when they encounter a situation that falls outside the scope of the task they have been designed for (their problem space).

## 62. Protecting intellectual property 1

1 Intellectual property is a unique creation of the human mind, such as an invention or design.

2 All original works are protected by copyright, because copyright is an automatic process, whereas a patent must be registered to give an inventor exclusive right to the features and processes of their invention.

3 Using a creative commons licence will allow Dave to give permission for other people to use his images. It will also allow him to specify any conditions on their use that he wishes to impose.

4 The logo identifies the company's goods and services to consumers, and so incorrect use of the logo could harm the company's reputation.

## 63. Protecting intellectual property 2

1 (a) Proprietary software is software that is owned by an individual or a company. Its source code is protected by copyright law, which makes it illegal for users to modify or distribute it.

 (b) The source code reveals how the program works. By keeping it a secret, developers prevent users from tampering with the code and stop competitors from stealing the ideas behind the code to use in their own programs.

 (c) Your answer could include one of the following:
 * The software will have been carefully tested, so Ibrahim is unlikely to encounter any bugs.
 * Technical support will be provided by the vendor, so Ibrahim can seek help if he gets stuck.
 * There will be plenty of books, magazine articles and online tutorials, so Ibrahim can use them to discover new features of the software.

## 64. Threats to digital systems 1

1 (a) Malware is short for malicious software. Such software is intentionally designed to cause damage or disruption to a digital system, or to gain access to sensitive data.

 (b)

| Characteristic | Virus | Worm | Trojan |
|---|---|---|---|
| Self-replicates | ✓ | ✓ | |
| Human action required to spread | ✓ | | ✓ |

2 The hacker can trick a user into downloading and running a Trojan by disguising it as legitimate software. Once installed, the Trojan will run automatically every time the computer is switched on, enabling the hacker to access files stored on the hard drive and providing a backdoor to other devices connected on the same network.

## 65. Threats to digital systems 2

1 (a) A technical vulnerability is a hardware, software or configuration fault that leaves a digital system vulnerable to attack.

 (b) Software with a known security bug that has not had a patch applied.

 (c) New security features are continually being introduced to combat new malware and other forms of attack.

2 Your answer may cover some of the following:
 * Using port scanning, hackers can find out which software and services are running on a computer and so identify any with known vulnerabilities.
 * Using port scanning, they can send data packets to specific ports and analyse the responses. This allows them to detect open ports that they can use as possible access points.

## 66. Threats to digital systems 3

1 Social engineering is an attack that exploits the way in which people behave and respond. It is used to trick people into either revealing sensitive information or downloading malware onto a computer.

2 (a) A pretexting attack is when the attacker pretends to be from a known and trusted organisation and uses an invented 'pretext' to contact the victim. They try to get the victim to divulge confidential information, often by creating a sense of urgency.

 (b) A quid pro quo attack is when the attacker offers the victim a service, such as a free software upgrade, and offers to help them install it. In exchange, the victim is tricked into divulging confidential information and/or permits the attacker to take control of their computer.

3 It enables attackers to gain access to confidential information without needing to have any technical expertise. People are also potentially more vulnerable to being tricked than computers.

## 67. Protecting digital systems 1

1 Sensitive data should be encrypted so that, should it be stolen, the thieves will not be able to understand it.

2 Both the sender and recipient use the same key to encrypt and decrypt the data.

3 (a) The signature library stores the signature patterns of known viruses. Incoming files are checked to see if they contain any of the signature patterns stored in the library, any that do are quarantined.

   (b) This type of anti-malware uses signature-based detection to identify malware whose signatures are stored in its signature library, and it uses behaviour-based methods to recognise any new malware whose signature has yet to be added to the library.

## 68. Protecting digital systems 2

1 (a) An AUP is used to set out what is and what is not permissible user behaviour. It is also used to spell out what will happen to anyone who breaks the rules.

   (b) By signing an AUP, employees are acknowledging that they have read the policy and that they agree to abide by it. The signed document can therefore be used in any future legal action against an employee who violates the company's rules.

2 The organisation can retrieve its data from the most recent backup copy that was made. This data can be reinstated on the company's computer system, once the damage in the server room has been repaired.

## 69. Decomposition and abstraction

1 Your answer code should include/do the following:
- Accept input of name as data type string.
- Accept input of age as data type integer.
- Completion of if statement with (theAge < 3).
- Completion of first elif with (theAge > 19).
- Addition of else for printing "can go to school".
- Addition of printing goodbye message as last instruction in file.
- Functions correctly for all integer input.

For solution see **69 Decomposition and abstraction 1 Model Answer.py**

2 Your answer code should include/do the following:
- Correct relational operators for at least one complete range check (both bounds).
- Correct Boolean operator for at least one compound test.

- Two inputs accepted.
- Calculation translated accurately.
- <string>.format() used to display distance.
- Distance displayed with no more than two decimal places.
- Levels-based solution design. You can find all the levels-based mark schemes on the Pearson website.
  - The problem has been decomposed using if/else rather than multiple ifs.
  - The correct use of data types is shown with conversion of inputs to float data type.
  - The logic is clear with message texts that are fit for purpose and suitable for the audience.
- Levels-based programming practices:
  - Effective comments explain logic.
  - Meaningful variable names have been used throughout.
  - White space is used effectively to lay out code for clarity.
- Levels-based functionality:
  - The solution interprets and executes demonstrating functionality.
  - The solution responds predictably for normal, erroneous and boundary data.
  - The solution demonstrates robustness within context of problem by keeping invalid data out.

For solution see **69 Decomposition and abstraction 2 Model Answer.py**

## 70. Read, analyse and refine programs

Your answer code should include/do the following:
- Variable layout amended to align headings with column content, e.g. "{:<10} {:>7} {:>6.1f}".
- Display separator line after column headings, e.g. print ("-"*30).
- Decimal argument to display percent to one decimal place in column, e.g. {:>6.1f}.
- Decimal argument to display percent to two decimal places in total, e.g. {:>6.1f}.
- Calculate total votes inside loop by changing "totalVote = totalVote + row[2]" to "totalVote = totalVote + row[1]".
- Outputs fit for purpose and suitable for the audience.
- Comments explain the logic.

For solution see **70 Read, analyse and refine programs Model Answer.py**

# 71. Convert algorithms 1

Your answer code should include/do the following:

- Initialise today, month and day to empty string.
- Initialise age to integer.
- Initialise height to real/float.
- Prompt and take string input for today, month and day.
- Prompt and take float input for height.
- Prompt and take integer input for age.
- Print today, day and month on same line.
- Divide height by age.
- Print result of division.
- Functions properly for all anticipated input.

For solution see **71 Convert algorithms 1 Model Answer.py**

# 72. Convert algorithms 2

Your answer code should include/do the following:

- Set setting to 0.
- Prompt for input indicates choice of 1, 2 or 3.
- Convert input of string to integer.
- Store input in setting.
- Use of if...elif...elif...else for checking options.
- Test conditions are ==.
- Every message matches test condition.
- Use of comment to explain logic.
- Meaningful identifier names.
- Functions correctly for all integer input.

For solution see **72 Convert algorithms 2 Model Answer.py**

# 73. Convert algorithms 3

Your answer code should include/do the following:

- Import random library.
- Set choice to empty string.
- Set number to 0.
- While loop used.
- Test condition is choice != "Q".
- random.randint() library function used.
- Range on random number is (1, 100).
- If...else selection used for even and odd.
- Modulus by 2 equals 0 is condition.
- Even and odd messages match test conditions.
- Variables have meaningful names.
- At least one comment is used to explain logic.
- Functions correctly by displaying all times tables results.

For solution see **73 Convert algorithms 3 Model Answer.py**

# 74. Convert algorithms 4

Your answer code should include/do the following:

- for in range used for outside loop.
- Range values of 1 and 13 for outside loop.
- Displays "Times table for <number1>" message.
- for in range used for inside loop.
- Displays "<number1> times <number2> is <number1 × number2>".
- Variable names are meaningful.
- Functions correctly by displaying all times tables results.

For solution see **74 Convert algorithms 4 Model Answer.py**

# 75. Convert algorithms 5

Your answer code should include/do the following:

- Initialisation of likes to empty list.
- Initialisation of total to 0.
- for ... in used to iterate over varieties, to prompt for user input.
- String concatenation used to create prompt.
- Conversion of response to upper case using <string>.upper ().
- Selection to check for Y.
- On Y, the variety is appended to likes.
- Variable for total is incremented on each Y response.
- Format of output uses string.format().
- for each used to iterate over likes, to create output string.
- Outputs fit for purpose and suitable for the audience.
- Comments explain the logic.
- Levels-based functionality:
  - Component parts of the program are complete and it is fully functional.
  - Outputs are accurate and messages are suitable for the audience.
  - Responds predictably to input of Y.
  - Functions without error in the context of the problem, as no validation was required.

For solution see **75 Convert algorithms 5 Model Answer.py**

# 76. Readability

Your answer code should include/do the following:

- The variable o is changed to a more meaningful identifier related to the user choosing the menu option.
- The variable r is changed to a more meaningful identifier related to radius.

- Importing of math library moved into a section for libraries.
- All constant (AREA, CIRCUMFERENCE, EXIT, NUM_OPTIONS) initialisations moved into a section for constants.
- All global variables (choice of menu option, radius) moved into a section for global variables.
- All subprograms (showMenu(), getUserOption()) moved into a section for subprograms.
- Layouts of code sections (libraries, constants, global variables, subprograms, main) have identifiers or titles as comments.
- At least four comments are used to explain the logic.
- At least four white spaces are used to aid readability.
- Functions correctly for anticipated input data.

For solution see **76 Readability Model Answer.py**

## 77. Program errors

Your answer code should include/do the following:
- Syntax – add double quote to gender list item.
- Syntax – add : to end of WHILE statement.
- Syntax – change ese: to else:.
- Meaningful identifier for gender list.
- Meaningful identifier for count and count2 such as female and male.
- Runtime error – change <= to < to avoid IndexError.
- Logic error – change print(index) to print(female).
- Readability – add some white space to separate variables from main program.
- Readability – add meaningful comment to explain logic.
- Functionality – working solution.

For solution see **77 Program errors Model Answer.py**

## 78. Fitness for purpose and efficiency

Your answer code should include/do the following:
- Multiple pepper variables reduced to a data structure (list) of any dimension.
- Multiple pepper variables reduced to a two-dimensional table of records.
- Pepper data structure ordered alphabetically by name to facilitate future searches.
- Multiple if statements to find a space changed to a loop.
- Loop structure for finding a space uses for instead of while.
- Finding maximum Scoville rating loop, incorporated into same loop as finding a space.

- Multiple if statements for printing out hottest pepper changed to be a single print statement at end of a loop.
- Levels-based functionality:
  - Components parts of the program are complete and it is fully functional.
  - Outputs are accurate and messages are suitable for the audience.
  - There is no input required.
  - Functions without error in the context of the problem.

For solution see **78 Fitness for purpose and efficacy Model Answer.py**

## 79. Structural components of programs

1  Your answer code should include/do the following:
- GREEN/PINK
- colour
- lineTable
- chooseColour
- doLine
- pTurtle/pX/pY/pAngle/pLineLength
- pTurtle/pX/pY/pAngle/pLineLength/choice/theColour
- 39–40
- 57–58
- 42-45

For solution see **79 Structural components of programs 1 Model Answer.py**

2  Your answer code should include/do the following:
- random
- MAX_SIDES
- rollDie()/getSides()
- welcome()
- pSides
- theFace/sides
- 41–43
- 43

For solution see **79 Structural components of programs 2 Model Answer.py**

## 80. Iteration

Your answer code should include/do the following:
- Use of at least one for each loop, which could be on either data structure to address items.
- Use of indexing to find the associated entry in the other data structure.
- Calculation of percentage of students enrolled on each language:
  - Dividing number by ON_ROLL.
  - Multiplying by 100.

- Use of round() function to reduce to two decimal places.
- Use of str() to convert real numbers (percentages) to strings.
- Use of concatenation to construct output strings.
- Variable names are meaningful in the context of the problem.
- Functions correctly to produce the values shown.
- Use of any comments to explain the logic.

For solution see **80 Iteration Model Answer.py**

# 81. Repetition

Your answer code should include/do the following:

- Choice of while (loopCount != 0):
- Choice of currentMax = -1
- Choice of currentMin = 999
- Choice of while (userInput != -1):
- Choice of print ("Avg number: " + str (total /countScores))
- Choice of loopCount = loopCount – 1
- Functions correctly for anticipated inputs.

For solution see **81 Repetition Model Answer.py**

# 82. Structured data types

Your answer code should include/do the following:

- Creation of two-dimensional data structure for storing data.
- Use of for … in to iterate in shortSeason().
- Use of at least one if statement for checking month range.
- Use of if with Boolean and for compound test for checking month range.
- Use of for … in range() loop to iterate in mediumOnly().
- Use of at least one if statement for checking sizes.
- Use of if with Boolean and for compound test for checking sizes.
- Levels-based functionality:
  - The component parts are clear, with the loops being clearly distinct from the selection statements.
  - The different outputs for the user are clear and they cannot be confused because there is a sentence indicating which is short season and which is medium sized only.
  - There is no input required to the program other than the internal data structures.
  - The program is robust; it translates and executes.

For solution see **82 Structured data types Model Answer.py**

# 83. Data types, variables and constants

Your answer code should include/do the following:

- Import math library.
- Create a constant using KIBI = 1024.
- Declare a number variable using int().
- Initialise the number variable to any integer.
- Create a variable for size in kibibytes, using a meaningful identifier.
- Set variable for size to any real value.
- Assign input value to number variable created above.
- Translation of formula uses constant defined above.
- Translation of formula is correct.
- Size in kibibytes used in call to math.ceil().

For solution see **83 Data types, variables and constants Model Answer.py**

# 84. String manipulation

Your answer code should include/do the following:

- Use len() to check length of input string.
- Use userInput.isalnum() to check for invalid characters.
- Set letters to first two characters of userInput.
- Use userInput.isalpha() to check for alphabetic characters only.
- Reversed test (not, == False) for alphabetic characters only.
- Use <string>.isupper() to check for upper case.
- Use <string>.islower() to check for lower case.
- Set digits to last three characters of userInput.
- Use <string>.isdigit() to check for all digits.
- Reversed test (not, == False) to check for all digits.

For solution see **84 String manipulation Model Answer.py**

# 85. Input and output

Your answer code should include/do the following:

- Import math library for use of floor().
- Use of constants for pass, fail.
- Calculation of mean is sum of tests divided by four.
- Use if if…else for determining pass/fail outcome.
- Use of <string>.format() for printing each student.
- Mean is displayed to two decimal places.
- Levels-based solution design:
  - Use of for loop to iterate over entire data structure.
  - Use of for or while loop to iterate over test grades.

– Resetting variable of running total for each student.

– Logical decomposition of separate tasks.

– Variables are appropriate types.

• Levels-based programming practice:

– Meaningful variable names.

– Some comments to explain logic.

– Layout separates constants, variables and program.

• Levels-based functionality:

– Functions for any number of records in the table.

– Produces the correct result for each student (given in question paper).

– Table design is fit for purpose and suitable for audience.

For solution see **85 Input and output Model Answer.py**

## 86. Read files

Your answer code should include/do the following:

• Opens the file in read mode.

• Uses a loop (for each, while not end of file) to read in every line.

• Removes the line feed using <string>.strip().

• Separates the line into fields using <string>.split(",").

• Appends each field to a new record.

• Converts data types (int) and (float).

• Calculates inventory cost and appends to record.

• Inventory is rounded to two decimals using round().

• Appends new record to data structure.

• File is closed.

For solution see **86 Read files Model Answer.py**

## 87. Write files

Your answer code should include/do the following:

• Open file before using file.

• Output line is constructed in order of [0], [1], [2].

• Addition of comma to output line follows addition of each field (twice).

• Calculation of total inventory using multiplication done inside loop.

• Rounding of total done after calculation of total.

• Concatenation of total done before addition of line feed.

• Line feed concatenated to output line just before writing.

• Writing of output line is last instruction inside loop.

• Close file before exiting program.

• Functions correction.

For solution see **87 Write files Model Answer.py**

## 88. Validation

Your answer code should include/do the following:

• isValidSandwich:

– len() has been used to find length of sandwich.

– Bounds on length match relational operator, i.e. >=3, <=20; >2, <21.

– Boolean operator(s) used to generate a valid test.

Example: ((len (pSand) >= 3) and (len (pSand) <= 20)).

• isValidMonth:

– Bounds on month are <1 and >12 (or equivalent).

– Boolean operator used is or.

Example: (not ((pMonth < 1) or (pMonth > 12))).

• checkPresence:

– Test is against empty string or length of 0.

Example: (choice == "") / (len (choice) == 0).

• isValidAxis:

– Bounds on range are >="X", <="Z" or equivalent.

– Boolean operator and relational operators generate a test for valid.

Example: ((pAxis >= "X") and (pAxis <= "Z")).

• userInput test:

– userInput != "Y", or equivalent.

• Functions correctly for all anticipated inputs.

For solution see **88 Validation Model Answer.py**

## 89. Pattern check

Your answer code should include/do the following:

• While loop checks for index less than length of SPECIAL.

• While loop keeps going for location equal to –1, i.e. not found.

• Argument to <string>.find() call is SPECIAL[index].

• Subprogram is called with argument of passKey.

• Characters before special symbol copied with range() values of 0.

– and symbolLocation.

• Characters after special symbol copied with range() values of symbolLocation+1.

– and len(passkey).

• Check for alphanumeric is temp.isalnum().

- Program functions correctly for anticipated input.

For solution see **89 Pattern check Model Answer.py**

# 90. Authentication

Your answer code should include/do the following:

- Length check on string password.
- Works for any length table as loop depends on len(userTable).
- Use of Boolean flag to stop search if found.
- Use of test and flag to stop search if position passed over.
- Biscuit question asked only if found.
- Error messages are informative and precise.
- Levels-based solution design:
  - Decomposition of inputs, processes and outputs clear.
  - All parts of the problem are addressed.
  - Use of while instead of for loop to allow early exit if found or passed over.
- Levels-based programming practice:
  - Meaningful variable names.
  - Comments explain the logic.
  - Constructs chosen to suit the problem.
- Levels-based functionality:
  - Fully matching information is authenticated.
  - "Record not there" is reported.
  - Unmatched record fields, not authenticated.

For solution see **90 Authentication Model Answer.py**

# 91. Arithmetic operators

Your answer code should include/do the following:

- Display suitable headers.
- Display a separator, using string multiplication.
- Use iteration (for) to access each item in the table.
- Calculate the length of the hypotenuse:
  - At least one use of exponentiation to power of two.
  - Use of square root/exponentiation to power of (1/2).
  - Translation of formula is completely accurate.
- Hypotenuse is rounded to two decimal places.
- Translation of area formula is completely accurate.
- Each record is displayed in a format fit for purpose using <string>.format().
- Program functions correctly and displayed results match those given in question.

For solution see **91 Arithmetic operators Model Answer.py**

# 92. Relational operators

Your answer code should include/do the following:

- Complete while with == "Y".
- Accept input with an appropriate prompt.
- Convert temperature input to integer.
- Complete if with temp > 30.
- Complete elif with temp > 5.
- Complete else with Just right.
- Functions correctly for all anticipated input.

For solution see **92 Relational operators Model Answer.py**

# 93. Logical operators

Your answer code should include/do the following:

- while loop completed with choice == "Y".
- Leaf colour completed with (colour < 1) or (colour > 3).
- Leaf size completed with (size < 1) or (size > 2) or equivalent expression.
- Leaf state completed with (state >= 1) and (state <= 2) or equivalent expression.
- Tip colour completed with (tips >= 1) and (tips <= 2) or equivalent expression.
- Nitrogen completed with colour == COLOUR_YELLOW.
- Magnesium completed with tips == TIPS_YELLOW.
- Calcium completed with state == STATE_CRACKED.
- Potassium completed with (colour == COLOUR_BROWN) and (size = SIZE_NORMAL).
- Phosphorous completed with (colour == COLOUR_BROWN) and (size == SIZE_SMALL).

For solution see **93 Logical operators Model Answer.py**

# 94. Subprograms

Your answer code should include/do the following:

- Import of time library.
- Use of range() to generate ASCII codes.
- Arguments for range are 90, 64, −1.
- Use of chr() function to find printable character.
- Use of time.sleep() to control timing.
- Argument to time.sleep() is 1.
- Accept a letter from the user.
- Validate the letter for lower case alphabetic only.
  - Note: this can be done with a range check (>= a and <= z) or string functions (<string>.isalpha() and <string>.islower()).
- Use of ord() to find code for letter.

- Accept a value from user.
- Convert value to real using float().
- Use of math.sqrt() or **(1/2) to find square root of real value entered.
- Use of round() to round to 4 decimal places.
- Use of str() to convert code and rounded number to string output.
- Use of concatenation for all output strings.

For solution see **94 Subprograms Model Answer.py**

## 95. Functions

Your answer code should include/do the following:

- Subprogram for counting spaces:
  - Takes one input parameter.
  - Use of for or while loop to iterate over the string.
  - Use of if and == to identify space character.
  - Increment count for space.
  - Return count of space to calling program.
- Subprogram for counting vowels:
  - Takes one input parameter.
  - Use of for or while loop to iterate over the string.
  - Use of if with Boolean operator to make compound test for vowels/use of in set of vowels.
  - Increment count for vowels.
  - Return count of vowels to calling program.
- Subprograms called with global variables.
- Displays number of characters, spaces and vowels.
- Levels-based functionality:
  - Translates and does not crash, even if there is limited functionality.
  - Input and output messages meet requirements of program.
  - Fully functional.

For solution see **95 Functions Model Answer.py**

## 96. Procedures

Your answer code should include/do the following:

- Definition of a subprogram to print column headers.
- Display headers subprogram takes no parameters.
- Display headers subprogram uses <string>.format() to display headers.
- Headers are fit for purpose and suitable to the audience.
- Definition of a subprogram to display each book.
- Display subprogram takes the table as a parameter.
- Each book printed using <string>.format().
- There is a call to the display headers subprogram, with no arguments.
- There is a call to the display books subprogram, with the table as an argument.
- Functions correctly without any additional input.

For solution see **96 Procedures Model Answer.py**

## 97. Local and global variables

Your answer code should include/do the following:

- Import of random library.
- One-dimensional list for storing flavours.
- Correct five flavours stored in list.
- Flavour chosen at random (using random.randint()).
- Use of only local variables, inside subprogram.
- Concatenation used in print statement.
- Functions correctly and produces the required output.

For solution see **97 Local and global variables Model Answer.py**